Role of social media in creating a new youth

Prakriti Jain

Department of Sociology

2022

LIST OF TABLE

CHAPTER: 1

TOWARDS SOCIOLOGY OF MEDIA:

A SOCIOLOGICAL DISCOURSE

INTRODUCTION

Today communication and information technologies have enabled the people to share the information instantly. Millions of people from almost everywhere in the world are connected to each other through these communication technologies that include various forms of mass media devices such as electronic media, Print media and the internet. It is called as Mass media because it helps to communicate with a large number of people instantly. These forms of media have undergone a rapid change. People can now read newspapers online just by installing an application in their mobile or laptop. Radio can now be listened on mobile phones .In order to stay connected with the friends and family members, people do not need phones now, only one smart watch will fulfil the need. This is known as media convergence[1]. In contemporary society, Internet plays an important role. Due to the impact of internet; people can gather information, entertainment and stay updated. William Gibson[2] in 1984 founded the term 'cyberspace' in his work 'Neuromancer'. Cyberspace is referred to as the space of communication which is formed with the help of global network which compose the World Wide Web. In cyberspace, people do not even have an idea or details about the people's identity, their gender or the place where they live. Modern society is characterized by the advent of internet which has created new virtual communities[3]. Virtual communities are a combination of a person's uniqueness and affability in modern network society[4]. This chapter gives a detailed account of media and its forms and the way it impacts the contemporary society.

1.1 MEDIA AND ITS FORMS

In this global age, mass media plays an important role .Mass media is a platform through which people communicate with the entire world. Almost every individual of

1

the society is making use of media in various forms like television, newspapers, radio and the internet. Mass media is an inseparable part of the people's life now. In this century, it is easy to disseminate the news and information with millions of people anywhere and everywhere in the world. Mass media is an effective tool for communication, advertising, marketing, buying and selling, sharing views and photos and videos.

According to McLuhan, modern media tend to create a global village in which people throughout the world see major events unfold together[5].

The world today is interconnected because people experience same event at the same time. This is due to the process of globalization and the advent of technology and communication .This has allowed the people of India and USA to experience each event together. Films which are made in South India are easily accessible to the people of North India. All these technologies have undergone a massive upgradation. For e.g.: -Newspapers can be read online now.

Features and forms of media:-

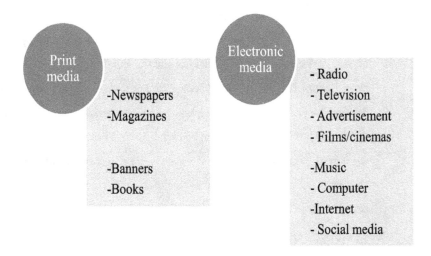

Print media
-Newspapers
-Magazines

-Banners
-Books

Electronic media
- Radio
- Television
- Advertisement
- Films/cinemas

-Music
- Computer
-Internet
- Social media

1.1(a) Print Media

It is the oldest and main form of mass communication. It includes newspapers, magazines and other form of material which is in printed form. The contribution of print media in disseminating the information is commendable. It is characterized for doing the in-depth analysis and reporting.

Newspapers The best example of print media is newspapers. It collects edits and analysis the news and provides it in a printed form. A newspaper comprises of many types of information in a creative and limited manner about current affairs, entertainment and consumer goods.

Magazines are something which are published periodically often monthly or weekly and they consists of written essays, stories, poems, articles, pictures etc. There are various types of magazines such as children's magazines, women magazines, sports magazines, political and religious magazines also. Nowadays in the era of internet and Social media, people can download apps which facilitate the reading of magazines on the phone, laptop etc.

Banners are made on paper, cloth or wall and are used to propagate any issue or any logo also used to advertise something.

Books are generally a collection of papers with a text written on it which is bound together in one cover.

1.1(b) Electronic media

India has witnessed a revolutionary expansion of electronic media. It is a type of media in which the user requires electricity to access it. It can also be called as 'Broadcast media'. It includes television, radio, Computer, Internet. The developing country like India, where it is not possible for everyone to own a television .Radio is the easiest and the cheapest way to inform and entertain the people. The contemporary society is characterized by the electronics people have in their home because of its easiest availability. It is impacting the mindset, attitudes and choices of the people of present-day society. The various types of electronic media -television, radio and the

3

internet. They are all intertwined now. Radio and television are the two main components of electronic media which are touching our lives in one or the other manner.

Radio broadcasting started in India in 1927 with the help of two transmitters Bombay and Calcutta. It is the form of mass media which can address both illiterate and literate. It has a feature of low cost, accessible to almost everyone easily. People, regardless of their location, can listen to news, sports broadcasts, comedy shows and live music. Common man who cannot afford television can listen to radio and enjoy music and stay updated about the events which are happening in the society. Advertising on the radio with catchy slogans is much prevalent today. Radio has an immense impact on the culture of the society. It has also introduced the feature to educate the people. The farmers who live in extreme rural areas can now have full information about the farming and agriculture. Radio broadcast has changed the lifestyle of the people around the world.

Television is a combination of technological developments in the field of motion pictures, photography and the electronic camera. It is kind of interaction between the audience and the television. Television has entered in every household now. It affects each and every aspect of individuals' life now. Roger Silverstone (1993:3) writes:

Television accompanies us as we wake up, as we breakfast, as we have our tea and as we drink in bars. It comforts us when we are alone. It helps us sleep. It gives us pleasure, it bores us and sometimes it challenges us. It provides us with opportunities to be both sociable and solitary. Although, ofcourse, it was not always so and although we have had to learn how to incorporate the medium into our lives we now take television entirely for granted.[6]

People get affected by the TV emotionally and cognitively .There are various media theorist who have critical views about the TV. This means that television is the form and it has some serious content. Print media has rational population, and the medium of television has the entertainment objective. The society dominated by television, radio and internet because it fulfils the objective of entertainment .From the beginning of the twenty-first century, there is an invention of digital television. **Advertising** is another form of electronic media which is used to communicate business/product information to the targeted customers. Basically it is the means of mass selling and buying that has increased up and is necessary for the mass production. In the era of television, radio and other forms of media the sellers cannot think of increasing their sale without the use of advertisement. In the present society, **Cinemas** also play an important role in bringing out changes in the society. It is the most important and popular medium of mass communication. Films reflect the circumstances, cultural trends which are taking place in the society. The moral values which are conveyed through the medium of cinema leaves a profound effect on the masses. The movies with the social lesson help to inculcate social values among the people. **Music** are the soul of any society; India has not been an exception to this. The Indian recorded music industry began in 1907 in Calcutta. The first recording of Indian song took place in 1902 in Bombay. Since its beginning, music continued to impact people's life and actions. In the era of Internet, music can be accessed easily and feasibly by watching or listening it on the YouTube. **Computer** is said to be a device that stores, retrieves and processes data which is composed of hardware and software. After the advent of computers, then came the internet (it is global set of interconnected computers).The spread of **Internet** facilities in almost every household led to the constant interconnection between the people. In contemporary society, the society is connected with a global system called **Internet.** World Wide Web is said to be the best known use of internet which was invented by Tim Berners-Lee. The browsers available on the internet which facilitates users to find any information. Nowadays the web also provides facilities for e-commerce. With the spread of cheap and easy availability of computers it is now easier to access the internet at home.

Impact of internet

The advent of internet is representing a networked global society. It has brought new patterns of sociability, interaction, consumption and employment opportunities. However, the most important use of internet nowadays is to access Social media. Use of internet also facilitates interaction with each other in the virtual space (cyberspace) even though they are unaware of the identity, gender or location of the person with whom they are interaction. Kolker argues that:

In our relationship with traditional media, we are always aware that what we read, hear and see has some kind of authorship behind it: someone writing and editing the newspaper column; producing, directing, and distributing a recording ,a radio or TV show, or a movie. Advertising reminds us continuously that someone wants something from us. But at the keyboard and online, we seem to be in control and in intimate connection with something or someone, in a world both internal and external simultaneously[7].

The advent of internet will bring new patterns of employment opportunities, sociability. The basic use of internet nowadays is due to the use of social media.

Social media

Social networking phenomenon has entered into the picture in past ten to fifteen years and it has grown from niche to a mass online activity in which millions of users are engaged. Today Social networking through internet sites is gaining popularity. It has altered the shape and form of social networking which was earlier a face-to-face phenomenon. Today Social media sites like Facebook, Twitter, Instagram, Myspace. The swift espousal of social networking sites is creating a subculture among today's youth. Sites like these are a common destination for all the people nowadays. Throughout people are creating their profiles publicly announcing their relationships with their partners and their current life happenings.

"Social media" are a group of internet based application that is build on the ideological and technological foundations of web2.0 which allows the creation and exchange of user-generated content.

History and origin of Social media

In the late 1990s internet became more prominent .It witnessed the appearance of those websites which allowed the users to create and upload content. The first Social network site was "SixDegrees.com" (1997). This was the time when texting got popular and people could create their own profile and foster friendship. A site called "Friendster[8]" came into existence. In its starting months only it got registered with three million clients. After this site many other Social networking sites such as LinkedIn, tribe.com began to pop-up. Soon in 2005 Facebook was launched. Unlike other Social networking sites Facebook provides feature to the users to keep their display picture as public or private. There are over 2.01 billion monthly active users on Facebook. Sites like these have given rise to virtual communities. Virtual communities are different from the traditional. People live in "multiple realities".People who use internet are called "netizens" and they have formed two identities –first in real world and the other in virtual world. The internet brings the people together, but due to it also keeps the people anonymous in communication.

The combining of new method of communication with new technology profoundly reshapes the ways by which people communicate with one another. The changed form of interactivity is the main feature to understand new media. The development of social media sites is place where artist can share their work and reach out with the whole world .With the help of the social media one can see a friend's new born baby on Facebook or can read people's view on demonetisation. The new media has created a virtual reality. It has an immense impact on the world. There are various kinds of social media like *Facebook* launched by MarkZuckerberg in Feb2004, launched a website *www. Facebook.com* has changed the form of interaction forever. People can create their profiles, add people in their friends lists, can exchange messages, pictures and videos. Today Facebook has become the most widely used social networking site in the world. People can create or join interest groups and can also "like pages" of their choice. Keeping in view the privacy of the users, it also has facility to choose their own privacy options and choose who can see their updates and posts. *Twitter* is owned by Twitter Inc. This enables its users to send and read messages and posts statuses which are called as tweets[9]. The users can subscribe to the other persons status update/tweets-following. And can posts their status using *hash tags #.Linked in* is a social networking site which is totally business oriented. It is mainly used by professionals. *You Tube* is a website which facilitates users to upload, new videos. People can also subscribe to the videos. This feature of video sharing is now said to be the most important factor of Internet culture. *WhatsApp* is an instant messaging application for Smartphones. It facilitates its users to send text, send and receive pictures, share videos and audios, group chats, location and share contact information. Recently a concept of WhatsApp Web was also introduced. Social media is used by people for variety of purposes such as social and professional. The rapid increase of use of internet in the mid 1990s has lead to the proliferation of virtual communities. Social networking sites are rooted in the everyday lives of the people and it influences on various aspects of life have changed the way of people's living way now.

- **Social Media and Education**

As the technology is developing the accessing of Social media is made easy because it can be used anywhere at any anytime. In the field of education, this technology is being used innovatively. In the educational institution students are taught to use this in a better way. With the help of Facebook students can share class notes with each other. They can easily learn any topic by watching it on video classes. Nowadays many coaching institutes offer video classes for the students. Teachers can create a group on Facebook and can post class assignments on it. There are several apps that offer social media in educational field. Using sites like Facebook in educational contexts can motivate the students and can attract them in learning. Using Google in the context of education is helpful. But on the other hand; it has certain negative effects also on the students. Students totally rely on the internet for spell check feature this is affecting their English language and their writing skills. Students nowadays try to multitask i.e., while studying use social networking sites on another tab shows reduced academic performance which reduces their ability to concentrate. Social media can prove to be very useful if it is used effectively but it can also be a distracting tool for the students. The easy access of social media gives the opportunities for the educators to teach good digital citizenship and using the internet productively.

- **Social media and Politics**

As the participation of people on social media in increasing it has become easy to disseminate the information using it. Many people use it to participate in social issues. Apart from using Social media for interacting, users also use it for various movements, it is also important for activists. Social has impacted almost each and every aspect of human life. It is a new tool for various political strategists and leaders of political parties. As the Social media gets deeply penetrated in the society, people are constantly connected to the politics, political parties and politicians. Almost all the political parties and politicians have their account on Twitter, Facebook and Instagram .Nowadays; only a tweet of 140 words can provoke and create a mass revolution. Earlier there used to be "war", "cold war" but now there is a new kind of war called as "twitter war". Various ministers express their views and arguments on twitter. In the present scenario common man can also participate in social media campaigns. It is also helpful for the voters to know which political candidate is better. Many young voters these days access political information before voting on the social networking sites .It has also given chance to the politicians to interact directly with the voters. Narendra Modi (Prime Minster) of India is very highly popular amongst the public .He has got a very large number of followers. Twitter gives its users the facility to disseminate the information worldwide .This helps the public to stay updated due to use of Social media.

- **Social media, family relationships and communication**

The integration of Social media into social settings like family, household is affecting the interaction pattern among the family members. Sites like Facebook and whatsapp is leading to an increase in the interaction between the members of family and also with the people who live far away. It is definitely bringing the members from all over the world together and reducing the generation gap. The sharing feature on Facebook strengthens the relationship ties amongst the members of family because the members of the family have some common topic to talk about. After Globalisation people are migrating to other cities for the sake of jobs and businesses can also talk to each other easily through the sites like Skype, Facebook etc. which was not possible earlier with the use of traditional media (letters, telegram). But on the other hand, Social media sites are also leading to a growing privatisation among the members .Members of the family while sitting with each other are physically present with each other but mentally they are with the person with whom they are talking online. This is creating strained relationships between the family members. Kids nowadays check their phone's notifications or focus more on their social media account rather than finding what is happening in front of them. Families where both the parents are working their children are immersed badly in technology i.e., playing video games, watching videos etc. People prefer talking online rather than talking face-to-face.

- **Social media and healthcare**

Social media has almost affected all the domains of life. The users of Social media sites can also use it for health care. They can participate in online communities, ask advice from the experts. People post their requirements of blood on their Face book profile at the time of need. People can also search for the information of a particular disease. It also allows various physicians to answer many questions of the people online. People are also using Social networking sites for supporting health-related cause such as signing petitions against harmful-drugs. While Social media has certain advantages but it also has some disadvantages. People while searching for certain diseases self-diagnose themselves by seeing it on the internet.This is evident that social media is having a profound effect on healthcare systems, and it is important both in the developed and developing worlds. Healthcare service provider's face can provide better healthcare to a greater number of people, while consumers are able to use it to empower themselves, their families and their communities.

- **Social media and Religion**

With almost every domain of the society is being discussed on the Social media. Religion is also one of them. Somehow it has changed the way people practise religion. By using the platform of Facebook religious organisation are able to interact with its followers. When a user posts a picture or status on Facebook. It becomes viral to the mass audience. Many contexts are attached into one which creates problem in the society. In this era of Social media, people are free to posts their views on their Facebook or Twitter account. Recently a well-known Indian singer, posted on his Twitter account about "forced religion" .In almost 5 or 10 minutes this post got viral and gained controversies. He was criticized a lot for his statements. In today's society, there is no need for organising rallies and protesting .Only a "share" or "like" can create controversy or violence in the society. Some people deliberately use Facebook or Twitter by updating hatesspeech about other religions with an aim of provoking a violent backlash. In a country like India, where so many religions and different communities exists even a single statement against any religion can cause violent coercion. Sites like Facebook and twitter has made "sharing" more easily. People can share information about or views of anybody without involving that person. When a person "likes" a page it will show up in the "news feed" of the people who are added in his/her friends list. Similarly, if a person "comments" on any of the religious page that action will also show in the "news feed" of his friends. This leads to passing information about ones religious views and activities sometimes consciously sometimes unconsciously.

- **Social media and children**

Around the world most people enjoy spending time on the internet. Social media such as Facebook, Whatsapp facilitates connecting with friends, classmates. Due to the absence of self-regulation children are at the highest risk of social media. Parents use Social media limitlessly and are comfortable with the fact that their children are using social media and the online content and do not keep pace with the children .Through social media children can exchange their views, thoughts and interests. Apart from this parents lack a basic thinking that their kids are getting involved in their online lives that they forget about their offline lives with their parents. The conclusion is that there is a technical and knowledge gap between the parents and the children. Even though Facebook has an age limit of 13 years for using it. But minors give wrong age to use this site. The rapid increase in the use of Social networking sites is causing an immense change in the young users. The children born after the year 1990 know the world through the internet.

a) *Social media and grades*: Media benefits the children also by using the apps which facilitates the teaching of alphabets and numbers are effectively helpful in teaching the kids. At the time of examination students feel stressed but using such sites to do e-mail instant messaging helps them to keep in touch with their friends and revise the syllabus. But using these sites for longer time duration during exams can prove to be harmful for their grades.

b) *Agitation to face strangers:* In the era of social media children are meeting the strangers online. They feel comfortable in talking to strangers online rather than talking to the people they know face to face. There are people who do not feel comfortable in talking to the people they acquaint .People search for true friends on face book and many other social sites irrespective of the fact that where that person live, or the age of that person.

However, the impact of new media technologies has resulted in the children using more technological equipments.Many social networking sites display advertisements that target people on the basis of their browsing choice which influences the buying decisions of the children. Parents should be aware of what their children are doing online.Due to the limited self –regulation and unlimited peer-pressure children are under the risk of getting addicted to Social media.Social media is full of content that is inappropriate for the children and can influence them to risky behaviours. Parents should educate their children about the ways through which Social media users can steal their personal information.

- **Social media and old age people**

The use of Social media has grown dramatically all over the world and amongst the people of all age groups. The older aged people are embracing the new technology. Many old age people use social networking tools to maintain their relations with friends, family and their closed ones. Social networking sites can help the retired people reconnect with the people from their past. In the old age people have many health concerns for which the blogs related to health can be helpful. Proving to be the best platform for maintain the communication and sharing pictures, videos with their loved ones and also helps in maintaining pace with the present generation.

"Social media provides isolated individuals of any age group with a socializing outlet. It is not uncommon for the elderly in our society to feel as if they have lost their social voice, and the use of social media restores this voice, often times from the comfort of one's home. The value in maintaining this voice for the elderly individual is undeniable[10]" (Morrison, 2010)

The most common benefit of Social media is its feature to stay connected with the people all over the world. As the person gets older people tend to lose some members from their social network ties. They change their jobs, get retired. Due to which it becomes more difficult for them to stay in touch with the people they once knew. Social media enables them to send e-mail instantly within seconds to the people who live distantly. It makes easy for them to stay in touch with their grandchildren. The older people who feel isolated sometimes internet proves to be the best companion for them. Some companies are producing customized mobile phones for older person which includes emergency alarms and easy to use keypad buttons. In old age, they may feel lagging behind and sidelined. By using Social media they can access news also and can stay updated that can significantly help them feel connected to the community.

- **Social media and youth**

With the increase in the usage of Social media it has become part of people daily life. The emergence of social media can be called as a "cool tool" for the youth to stay connected with each other. In modern society, media is not only limited to the feature of broadcasting but also interactivity, multimedia and multitasking. Today messages can be sent to the people and the target people in real time they can create changes and tendencies. Because of technology crowds are becoming more powerful it has got the power to unite the people. Social media is a platform for the people to stay connected with the friends, reconnect with the old friends and can also create real life friendships with the people one has never met or with the people who is living far away by sharing similar interest, hobbies and views. All over the world people are spending much of their time on Social media through cell phones. The easy availability of mobile phones makes it easy for people to use Social media. This is increasing the number of user's day by day. Social media impacts the youth in almost every aspect of their life. Some of the effects (positive/negative) of Social media are given below:

- **Social Media: An evaluation**

Social networking sites offer a wide advantage of disseminating information to all the people which was not possible earlier while using the traditional media. It allows people to engage themselves in various activities from their home. With the help of internet people can shop online, pay bills, and can also search for specific information .The users of internet can also form online communities and groups with the people who have specialized relationships with each other .Just by sitting at home people have access to information of various categories such as: Politics, education, religion, fashion, social activities, recreational pleasures. Communities formed on the internet have ideal type of relationships because information can be posted anytime and response can be received very fastly. This gives its members a sense of belonging. Users can protest and can support any issue .It is simple and cheap to use. However, While the information posted on internet is disseminated fastly. But it is also posted

14

without being reviewed for correctness. As there is no editor on the internet it is difficult to judge what is right and what is wrong. On Social media identity is kept anonymous so it is easy for people to make fake accounts and live out in a fantasy as another type of person. Social networking sites such as Facebook and twitter makes people addicted to it. They spend lots of time which diverts them from doing an important task. Due to overuse of Social media family ties are weakening because people spend more time connecting to new people. Young people wastes most of their time which also affects their health.

1.2 THEORETICAL FRAMEWORK

1.2(a) Early Sociological theorists

- **Durkheim{1893(1933)}**[11] believes that as the society evolves and industrialization advances, the process of division of labour becomes important. Division of labour equates to specialization of labour; that leads to effective functioning of society which further leads to social progress. Specialization of labour demands assignment of specific roles to each that results in interdependence on each other because everyone is specialized in their own field .He gave the concept of social solidarity and its two major types-*Mechanical solidarity* and *Organic Solidarity.* Mechanical solidarity is characterized by common sentiments and beliefs of the people where people share same joys and same struggles due to homogeneity of society while *organic solidarity* results in integration due to specialization of labour.Mechanical solidarity is characterized by *repressive laws* and the organic solidarity by *restitutive laws.* In today's society, which is characterized by organic solidarity new techniques have developed for social interaction. Durkheim is interested in social solidarity, and today's society interacts and binds people through social media .Through Facebook, Twitter and whatsapp people are constantly connected to each other. This has changed the scenario today people connect through social media interact through it and due to social media there is a social bonding as well. Social media is the new means to develop organic solidarity. Restitutive laws in the form of 'cyber laws' exist to bring normalcy when society suffers from the threat posed by excessive and indiscrete use of Social media.

- **Weber (2006)**[12] introduced the term *rationalization* to explain the societies and their transformation from simpler to scientific form. It has replaced traditional thinking with rational thinking attitude which results in technological advancements. Weber viewed that rationalization would lead to dehumanized and alienated society where each individual would see their best means to achieve end. Weber focused on 'social status' which means the place which a person acquires in a society. In a technological society people are busy on social networking sites (Facebook, Twitter) which are also status-driven. Just by creating a profile on Facebook a person can present himself in a very creative manner. Weber was mostly concerned about 'iron cage' which was caused by the expansion of formal rationality. People are now caged in the cage of social media and are busy in their own phones and laptops .The humanly created Social media has begun to exert dominance over its creator. The motivation for human action in society changes from values, emotion and sympathy to rational calculations and efficiency.

- **Marx(2016)**[13] the concept of Alienation can rightly be used in the context of Social media .It happens in two ways- Because of Social media people now feel alienated because they are much more connected to the person with whom they are interacting through social media. And this has led the face-to face relations weaker day by day. People today are constantly talking with their friends on social media but in real life they feel alienated. People sometimes feel that they are over with the real-life interactions and their interaction with their online friends boosts them up. They spend most of their time on social media and also compare themselves to others and this is where alienation comes from because they feel that they cannot match up with the happening life that someone else portrays online.

• **Simmel(2011)**[14] has talked about social relationships in pre-modern and modern societies both. He analyses various relationships from the perspective of knowledge and secrecy. He viewed that the emergence of various interest groups is due to the objectification of culture so it requires less subjective totality amongst the individual. In pre-modern societies, people used to know each and every thing about their friends. But in modern societies, people have a little idea about their friends. He has talked about the relationship of friendsh*ip,* assumes that it is the bond which is full of intimacy and almost no secrets. But it is only possible in pre-modern societies because people have nothing to hide in that society. Modern society is a kind of specialized and differentiated society where interaction is mainly through social media and other forms .In modern society people have different interest in the field of religion, intellectual views, experiences. People only know limited information about the people they are talking with on Facebook .For eg. In modern societies people make fake account on Social networking sites and portray themselves as a different person .And the people who are added in their friends lists talk to them as the person which they present .In modern societies, there is little intimacy involved in the friendship and a large amount of secrecy.

• **Mead (2012)**[15] impetus is on "I" and "Me" and the 'self' in the social interaction. For him, a person is not born with a consciousness of self but it is developed from the social interaction with others "ME" refers to the social self and "I" is the response to me. While using Social networking sites such as Facebook, Twitter and Instagram there is continuous interaction between its users. Focusing on likes, comments and Tweets people measure ones self-esteem. While posting their pictures on Social media if people do not get enough likes it poses negative impact on their health. The users decide "what's on their mind" or while updating their status they create a representation of themselves or "me" based on their experience. He also talks about two types of "others": *significant others generalized others.* Significant others refer to the individuals which influence a person's perspective. Generalized others refers to the particular people who influences one's culture. Social media allows people to share their videos, pictures, views and life experiences on their profile. Every user is said to be an "actor" and others among the social media are "targets". These targets comprises of "generalized others". In the era of Social, media no comments or likes will lead to negative judgement of oneself but at the same time too many comments and likes will also lead to a positive sense of oneself. So, rather than developing a sense of self based on the opinions of the people in the physical environment or the people present in the real life or face-to-face interaction people depend on the friends or users present on the Social media to approve their life .

Veblen (2011)[16] The use of social media on internet has created online groups and communities which have promoted new social relationships and because of these communities and virtual groups people get to know about what is happening in the world. He has talked about conspicuous consumption in his work 'the theory of leisure class(1899)'.He argued that in order to make themselves look more rich and attractive people prefer using goods of higher quality and price. In modern society, people can portray themselves how influential, happening they are. And it doesn't even cost anything. People update their status about the places where they are going and it's a kind of culture in which they think that it will enhance their status amongst their family and friends irrespective of the fact that they visit those places or not. In the era of Social media, people portray the conspicuous side and have less privacy. Now the information has new controls which lead to unintended consequences.

- **Tonnies (2002)[17]** has talked about gesellchaft and gemeinschaft in which gemenischaft refers to the community which has face to face relations and the relations are informal i.e., the relations which are physical in nature. On the other hand, the other is gessellschaft which refers to association with formal relations and relations with motives and self-interests. In modern world, the relations which are made through social networking sites are gessellschaft in nature because most of them are not face-to-face relation and formal in nature. Since more and more people in the contemporary society are joining Social media, the community bonds are waning. The modern type of community is like Gesellschaft with almost little emotional ties .People are connected to each other through Facebook and other social networking sites but are not emotional involved with each other.

1.2(b) Modern sociological theorists

• **Giddens (1998)**[18] thinks that modern society is like a "juggernaut "which is the advanced stage of modernity and thinks that this juggernaut does not follow a single path and is made up of number of conflicting and contradictory parts. Today's society is under the domination of modern technology and the biggest achievement of technology is the introduction of internet which is moving along with time and physical space. In Giddens structuration theory there are three essential aspects distanciation, disembedding and reflexivity. The first one is *time and space* separation. Now we have more close relationships with those who are physically far away from us. Time and space separation or the process of distanciation. The second aspect is disembedding which involves 'the 'lifting out 'of social relations from local contexts of interaction and their restructuring across indefinite spans of time-space'. Thirdly, Take an example of LGBT rights Social media is widely used to spread the awareness of LGBT rights The mainstream media have their standards on gender issues and these topics are now allowed in the mainstream movies or shows .Therefore Social networking sites act as a alternative platform to publish such content. The use of social networking sites has promoted online interactions amongst the people. His thought of modernity has a runaway engine which has got many problems. In modern society, almost every transaction is done online which includes risks of theft .Many cyber stalkers are only present in the chance of getting all the bank details of the people and stealing peoples money. Due to the increased use of social networking sites the relationships with those who are physically far are closer than the people who are physically near. Because of social networking sites people can have friends all over the world now. Common interests and common goals are the main basis of thesis friendships. People now prefer selecting their mates and life-partners online through the sites like tinder, Facebook etc. He was mainly concerned with the new type of risk associated with the modern world and to deal with this new type of risk new kind of expert system is also required.

- **Beck (2016)**[19] compared modern society with 'risk' society. 'the prior "classical" stage of modernity was associated with industrial society, while the emerging new modernity and its technologies are associated with the risk society' 'As the society is becoming more and more global and techno savvy there are more chances of global risks. Now there are new types of problems associated with this information society. About 10 years ago there was nothing like 'cyber-crime' prevailing in the society. In earlier societies, it was the proletariat only who were 'vulnerable' and 'victimized' it modern society each and every person the under the risk of getting victimized.The weapon for bringing disaster can be advancement of technology and using it in a way which is harmful for the society. These risks which are created by the advance of science and technology are different from those of previous ages. Social media obviously provides many benefits to the people (as they are constantly connected to each other) .Yet the risks it creates is also hard to measure. With the advancement of Internet cyber crime has come into the picture. According to Beck, if any of the innovation of technology went wrong, then the consequences of it would be harmful for the society. Social media is an important domain for the social construction. But there are unlimited numbers of risk associated with it.

- **Ritzer (2016)**[20] based his ideas on Weber's theory of rationality. Weber focused on that in modern world the people are living in iron cage that gives more importance to rationality, efficiency. Similarly, Ritzer gave the concept of Mc Donaldization which is also a kind of formal rationality and has four major qualities:

- *Efficiency* to achieve best means to an end. Through Facebook information is disseminated in seconds. The information or the news also has multiple receivers.

- *Predictability* in which there is nothing new. Social media reminds the people about the important happenings of the users' life.

- *Rational system* which focuses more on quantity rather than giving good quality; People focus more on having friends online rather than having real-time friends.

- *Reliance* on technology. People nowadays are all dependent on Social networking Sites.

His model of mcdonaldization basically focuses on information society. Now one can search almost everything on the internet can buy something or sell something also. But advancement of technology is also a threat to society. The communication feature of Social media has made emotion as a thought of past.

- **Merton (2012)**[21] differentiated between two types of functions-*manifest functions* and *latent functions*. Manifest functions are those which are known and intended by the participants in any kind of social activity or interaction. And Latent functions are those which are not known and are unknown. Social networking sites perform both of these functions. Through Social media people stay connected to each other and are also connected to the whole world. But on the other hand it promotes loneliness amongst the people. Social media serves the function of status conferral. Social status of people is elevated when favourable attention is given to them on Social media. This not only enhances the prestige of the person but promotes it within wide circles of population. The social media may initiate organised social action in order to enforce the social norms. For e.g.:-signing of petitions. Merton has also talked about dysfunctional aspects of every element in the society. Social media also has some dysfunctional aspect in the society. People are well informed about everything on Social media but are not doing anything in reality .this has made the people apathetic and inert. It is so addictive that people spend most of their time on it and due to this people escape from their real-life relations.

- **Goffman (2013)**[22] in his work *Presentation of self in everyday life* (1959) talked about the similarities between theatrical performances and the acts of the people's day-to-day life. He saw much in common between the stage performances and the social interaction. He argued that in every interaction there is *a front region* and *back region*. Front region (social and public arena) is the place where people are conscious about their dressing style, fashion, appearance. Back stage (private realm) or region is the place where people can be behaving as themselves. While having online social interaction people also have two regions .People post on Facebook keeping in mind about their status and how it will appear on their profile. This can be the front stage and back stage can be their offline appearance. He was also interested in the gap which pertains between what a person shows he is i.e., *virtual social identity* and what a person actually is i.e., *actual social identity* .The person who is having this gap is said to be *stigmatized* .Stigma mainly focuses on the interaction between normal people and the stigmatized. He talks about two types of stigma -*Discredited stigma* in which the audience knows the differences about the actor. *Discreditable Stigma* is when the differences are not known by the actors. The users of Social media have both the kinds of Stigma attached with them. Social media is a platform where very little is known about the personality of an individual resulting in a society of indifference.

- **Friedan (1963)**[23] wrote about women's lives and their exploitation in domestic sphere 1950s. She discussed the 'problems with no name'. Because in domestic sphere there life is bound up in childcare, domestic works etc. She viewed that education and only education can save women from this exploitation. But in modern society, Social media is a tool for the feminist to promote feminism. The most powerful weapon is the "hashtag". Before the advent of social media the things like rallies were limited to the people who were in those cities and for those who can afford to take time from their busy schedule to participate in the rally. But soon after the introduction of Facebook and Twitter people can now afford to participate in the movement by simply creating a group or by writing a status using hashtag. India is also witnessing the # metoo movement in the past few

22

days. Social media has reduced the barriers of time and distance and has made activism easier. Therefore, Social media is the most widely used powerful tool for advocating women's rights.

1.2(c) Post- modern sociological theorists

Post modern Social theory is a new way of analyzing about post modernity. This society is characterized by the weakening of earlier culture and emergence of new culture and mostly youth is affected.

* **Baudrillard (2016)[24]** emphasized on the fact that the media alters people's perception of reality. In the modern world people live their lives in the realm of hyper reality connecting more with the Television; Mass media ,Internet or Social networking sites (Facebook, Twitter , Instagram and Snapchat).The coming of Internet or the Social media has changed the lives of the people. Social networking sites not only represent the 'world' .For example-Instagram is a Social networking Site which facilitates its users to upload a picture of them. Now the picture uploaded might have no link with the real life . He argues that in a society where Mass Media is present everywhere a new reality is created –*hyperreality* (mixing of people's behavior and media images) which has no connection with the reality. These Social networking sites are a simulation of reality because it makes a person believe it is real.

* **Castells (1996)[25]** views modern society featured by networks that connects the individuals around the world. These online ties have become so pervasive to the human beings that they have started altering the basic material conditions and affect almost every aspect of the society. Modern society is differentiated with the earlier society because it is governed with Information and Communication technology (ICT). The present society i.e., the network society is based on two phenomena-Technology and globalization. Through Social media one can search for employment opportunities, collaborations. Society dominated by networks is called Network society. He defined Network society as:(Castells, 2006:7)[26]

A social structure based on networks operated by information and communication technologies based in microelectronics and digital computer networks that generate, process, and distribute information on the basis of the knowledge accumulated in the nodes of the networks.

He focused on the interaction between networks in the society. A network society is one connected by series of networks through multiple nodes. He called this scenario as a new public sphere where society is connected globally. The ties which are made through this have become so important for the people that they have affected nearly every aspect of the people s life.

- **Habermas (2016)**[27] describes *public sphere* as an area where public debates and issues are discussed, which is important also for the smooth functioning of democracy in the society. In the earlier society' ssalons, coffeehouses, restaurants were the main public spheres where all the people would meet and discuss all the general issues with each other. In the modern age, Public sphere can be seen in the Social networking sites because it is the fastly growing arena of public debate now. People can posts almost everything on the social networking profile .Twitter is said to be the most used platform for public debates. Many people use it to share their views on various issues such as politics, entertainment, sports etc. The advent of internet has made it easy to reach large number of people ,which would have been difficult with the use of traditional media .It is made easy to connect with the people globally.

1.3(a) Sociological theories of Mass communication

The sociological approach to the theories of communication aims that there is a relationship between mass communication and the social changes which is prevailing in the society. Some relevant theories are:

- **The cultivation theory**

Developed by **George Gerbner**[28] in 1967. The theory assumes that the continuous exposure of media have effect on people and can also alter the perception of people.

24

Initially the theory was formed for analyzing the effects of TV. But in contemporary society, Social media plays an important role. People absorb the dominant images, styles and the messages of the people .According to it, constant acquaintance with the media is capable enough to cultivate common beliefs among the people. Social media has become major part of people's lives. They spend more time on Social media than at any other activity. It has dramatically changed the daily schedule of the people. He is of the view that constant usage of mass media leads to the 'cultivation' of its customs, culture in the people. They integrate it to their real-world perceptions and judgments'. He detected a process occurring which is termed as *mainstreaming,* whereby media creates a mixing of together. According to him, viewers use media to confirm the way things are. Media's images cultivate the tendencies which are dominant in nature such as culture's beliefs, ideologies and views.

- **Social learning Theory**

According to this theory, learning occurs through social context. It focuses that people learn from each other through observations, imitation and modeling. With the increasing use of Social media it is deemed capable of teaching its users both positive and negative behaviors'. Sites like Youtube facilitates uploading of videos (cooking, singning, make-up tips).People can learn from them. People observe the behavior patterns of his/her Facebook friends and copy them. Especially children try to imitate the stunts which are shown in the television or Youtube. The important component of this theory is that it analyses how people can learn from observations.

- **Agenda setting theory**

The term was coined by Maxwell McCombs and Donald L. Shaw in 1972. An agenda is defined as selection of some items to give more importance to them. According to this theory, the news media presents the news or the information to the public with the picture of the world as is but with an agenda of their own selection i.e., they select the report about what is happening in the world. The theory assumes that ifparticular news is presented frequently by the media the viewers will believe that it is important. Print media receives number of news but select only few of them. It is known as gate keeping. These results in giving emphasis to one news and others being enfolded. Thus gatekeeping results in a news agenda presented by the print media to the viewers. But in contemporary society, which is dominated by the internet. It has changed the scenario because now each and every news is available to the people easily. Today people have easy access to the national and international news through their Smartphone. Social media acts as a egalitarian platform because common man can determine issues of importance according to their wish. Now media has become personalized so it is in the hands of its users to decide which news has to be given importance. Just by downloading an app of a newspaper people can stay updated and informed about the global events. The advent of social media has completely changed the scenario. And this is challenging the Agenda setting theory.

- **Play theory**

Introduced by **Stephenson,** chose to focus on the positive aspects of media highlights that how people use media and how it is transforming and bringing changes in day to day life of the people. He viewed that media serve audiences as play experiences. Even newspapers are read for one's amusement rather than getting information. Communication pleasure is about how media provides people with a common interest so that they can interact with others .In the age of social media, people can interact with others even when they do not know each other but can interact about what is going on in the news channel.

- **Uses and Gratification theory**

This theory argues that media do not do things with the people rather it's the people who only do things with the media. In other words, nothing can influence the people if it has got "no use" of it for the users. Social media is used by the people for numerous reasons:

> It provides knowledge, information. Search engines on the internet like Google, Bing etc. is helpful in spreading knowledge and information nowadays social networking sites like Facebook and twitter also helps in communication about what is happening in the society.

➢ It satisfies their emotional needs.

➢ It also provides status to the user amongst their peers.

➢ It is the easiest way to interact with the family, friends and colleagues.

The influence of media is limited to what people allow it to be. This theory assumes that users are aware of their needs and can express them.

- **Dependency theory**

This theory assumes that people are dependent upon media to get information, meet needs. At critical times, people increasingly depend on media for information and guidance. At the time of demonetization, media was the most important medium to get information. Media offers its users the content which is highly authentic and it is able to fulfill the needs of the users. In industrialized societies, the dependence of an individual on any kind of media is developed to satisfy a variety of needs ranging from providing information of a political candidate or taking an idea of fashion in the market to a need for relaxation and entertainment. Nowadays on Facebook/ Instagram people can search for any celebrities and their personal information which was not possible with the use of traditional media. There are two factors which influence the degree of dependence on media. Firstly; people are only dependent on that type of media which will satisfy their needs than on the media which will satisfy only few of them. Secondly, when conflict and social change will take place in the society then reliance on the media will rise. During the Uttrakhand disaster, Whatsapp is used by many helpless people to locate a spot. This theory sets up a relationship between media, users and social system.

1.4 Towards Sociology of Social Media:

The contemporary society is marked by the advent of new cultural traits in the world society; most importantly the internet and social media that is accessible to a large audience. The excessive use of social networking sites has ushered in new life style patterns. It allows society to build and maintain relations on a global level, with immediate access to family, friends, relatives and community. It has altered the form of human communication; what began as an interaction between people has occupied a public domain. People are engaged in diverse activities on social media; from cultivating friends on Facebook to following and connecting with people on Twitter, Instragram and Whatsapp. While doing so, they constantly upgrade their profiles to maintain the interest of their friends and followers. Social media is also proving to be a financial asset for those engaged in businesses as it helps them to advertise as well as draw potential customers. Further, social media is becoming a growing platform for social awareness and political debates. In other words, social media has affected almost every age group of society who use it as a platform for diverse activities. It has driven the human communication to a level where face to face communication is neither important, nor necessary; as people all over the globe can be engaged through social networking sites. Such engagements facilitate new power dynamics where some are heard loud and better due to greater visibility. It is thus evident that social media has created a whole new sociological world that needs to be explored and revisited.

Notes and references

1. Media Convergence-The process in which different media forms merge in new ways. It was introduced by Jenkins .According to him; it is an ongoing process that should not be seen as an alternate of the old media, but it is the interaction between different media forms.

2. Gibson, William (1984), *Neuromancer*, Pg.4, Ace Hardcover, New York.

3. Virtual communities- The term was invented by Howard Rheingold in his work *The virtual community* as a community of people sharing common hobbies, interests, ideas and feelings on the internet. He also created one of the first major internet community named 'well'. These communities have no linkage with space and time.

4. Network Society-The term *network society* was coined in Norwegian by Stein Bratenin his book *Mode lleravmenneskeogsamfunn* (1981).After the term was

used in Dutch by Jan van Dijk in his book *De Netwerkmaatschappij* (1991) (*The Network society)*and by Manuel Castells in *The Rise of the Network Society* (1996).

5. McLuhan, M. (1964) *Understanding Media,* Routledge, New York.

6. Silverstone, Rogers (1994), *Television and everyday life*, Pg.778, Routledge, London.

7. Kolker, R. (2009) *Media studies: An introduction*, Wiley, Chichester.

8. Friendster-It is a social networking site which was designed to exchange views, text, pictures and videos by the users.

9. Tweets–These are written posts of up to 140 characters displayed on the users profile page (as defined by oxford dictionary).

10. Morrison, D. "Social media opens social world to elderly, disabled." Wilmington Star News. January 26, 2010.
    (http://www.starnewsonline.com/article/20100126/articles/100129755)\

11. Durkheim, Emile (1893/1933), *The division of labor in society*. Trans. by G. Simpson. New York: The Free Press.

12. Wallace, Ruth (2006), *Contemporary Sociological Theory, Pg. 170, Prentice* Hall of India, New Delhi.

13. Giddens, Anthony(2016), *Sociology,* Pg.796, John Wiley & Sons, New Delhi.

14. Ritzer, George (2011), *Sociological theory,* Pg.184, Tata McGraw Hill Education Private Limited, New Delhi.

15. Kundu, Abhijit (2012),*Sociological Theory,* Pg.126, Dorling Kindsley (India) Pvt. Ltd, Noida.

16. Fuchs, Christian(2015),*Culture and economy in the age of Social media,* Pg.13, Routledge, New York.

17. Ritzer , George (2011),*Sociological theory,* Pg.184, Tata McGraw Hill education Private Limited, New Delhi.

18. Loomis, Charles (2002),*Community and society,* Pg.5, Dover Publications, New York.

19. Tucker, Kenneth (1998), *Anthony Giddens and Modern Social theory,* Pg.185, Sage Publications, London.

20. Giddens, Anthony (2016),*Sociology,* Pg.451, John Wiley & Sons, New Delhi.

21. Ritzer, George (2016), *Essentials of Sociology,* Pg113, Sage publications India Pvt. Ltd, New Delhi.

22. Kundu, Abhijit (2012), *Sociological Theory,* Pg.101, Dorling Kindersley (India) Pvt.Ltd, New Delhi.

23. Cunningham, Carolyn (2013), *Social networking and Impression management,* Pg.37, Lexington Books, U.K.

24. Freidan, Betty (1963),*The Feminine Mystique,* Pg.388, Victor Gollancz, London.

25. Lovink, Geert (2016),*Social media Abyss: Critical Internet culture and the force of negation,* Pg113, Polity Press, U.K.

26. Castells, Manuel(1996), *The rise of network society,* Pg.293, M.A: Blackwell Publishers, Cambridge.

27. Castells, Manuel (2006), *The network society: from knowledge to policy*, Center for Transatlantic Relations: The Paul H. Nitze School of Advanced International Studies, The Johns Hopkins University, Washington.

28. Giddens, Anthony (2016), *Sociology, Pg. 793, John* Wiley & Sons, New delhi.

CHAPTER: 2

THE NETWORK SOCIETY, SOCIAL MEDIA AND EMERGENCE OF YOUTH SUBCULTURE: AN ANALYSIS

2.1 Introduction

The shift of society from agrarian to industrial and then information society has ushered in a new era where boundaries are disappearing. The boundless use of internet technology has already shrunken the world into a 'global village'[1]. The evolution of technology is shaping the values, attitudes, social relationships, and behavioral patterns of the people. Not surprisingly, young people have been the fastest to acquire the digital media traits and have employed them in their daily lives. The trends which newly emerge at any stage of society lead to future changes in the society. Society can be easily transformed by technology. Nodes and networks of connection are the main basis of post-modern society. With the use of networks, new opportunities can be created, but without its use the survival is very much difficult. Networks are basically a set of interconnected nodes, which promote financial and flows with the help of technologies. Almost all the developing and developed countries have witnessed the emergence of network society. Today there is a very thin blurred line between real and virtual world and due to which new possibilities are evoking in social and cultural realms. The advent of Internet has given rise to Social media which enables the people to stay connected with each other. The interactive feature of this media combined with cameras, search engines and notebooks leads to an increasing demand of communication devices. Users are connecting with the internet also to buy and sell resources, also to take classes (to learn or teach something), and to play online games. The increasing use of Social networking sites is an important feature of Network society and its excessive use is creating a new kind of subculture amongst the youth. This chapter examines the youth subculture which is emerging with the use of Social networking Sites.

2.2 NETWORK SOCIETY: A curtain raiser

The last two decades of 21st century witnessed structural changes in the society. The internet plays a crucial role in this process .With the advent of internet and mass communication, organizational and inter personal communication has become fast paced. More people are linked to one another and have constant access to information. Internet has brought the whole world closer, this is how the concept of Network Society emerged. The term was first used by Manuel Castells in Sociology. He used the term in his work *The Rise of The Network society*. Castells wrote that there is a shift of global society to informational and technological society in the past few decades[2]. Whereas industrial society was characterized by the advent of transport and machinery; and the network society is featured by the means of digital communication. It is characterized by the social structure which is established by new innovations and developments ICTs. The main basis of Network society is individuals and groups such as family, community and work are linked by networks. The three main factors responsible for the emergence of Network society are:

- In order to promote open market approach reconstitution of industrial economy was promoted.

- Certain movements such as Civil rights ,movement, feminism and environmental movements

- The humongous rise in Information and communication technology

Castells defined networks as the set of interconnected nodes which helps in processing financial and other valuable flows with the help of technology. He argued that the force of technology does not bring change in the society but the emerging changes in social needs leads to the development of technology. The main basis of Network Society is technology. The two major phenomena which influence Network Society are technology and globalization. The most common access mediums of network are mobile phones and Internet. They facilitate the use of Social networking sites easily. With the advent of new media (Facebook, Twitter, Instagram, Pinterest), horizontal and vertical communication has developed. The accessibility of technology at low cost also allows for mobility. As a result, it leads to diffusion of technology at anytime, anywhere and by anyone. Dr. NormanNie (2001)[3] argued that the advancement of technology affects youth's social life. The evolution of Network Society influences all aspects of society including Youth and their culture. Jan Van Dijk[4] argued that social networks assisted by the media networks are available at all the levels of society. They are exist at four levels:

1) First: The basic level is the level of individual relations corresponding to common sense meaning of social networking .Individuals create ties with family, friends and colleagues etc. Presently, this networking is linked with the emergence of new media network such as email, telephone and mobile.

2) Second: This level is linked with the relations takes that takes place at the organizational levels. Currently, the contemporary groupings are facilitated by telecommunication and computer networks resulting in virtual organization at each and every scale and loosens fixed groupings and organizational structure. However it has also resulted in the networking of organizations which also leads toh cooperation in the execution and implementation of particular tasks.

3) Thirdly, all the relations in the society are connected by social media networks.

4) As people are entering in the era of web, global relations have taken place which is ensured by computer networks.

The main characteristics of network society as given by Manuel Castells[5] are:

- There is transformation of sociability. People are getting isolated and face-to-face interactions are fading away.

- The most important key factor of network society is the information technology.

- Power rooted in networks spreads at all levels.

- Communication is not at all managed by time and space it is dependent on mobiles and other gadgets which are easily movable which is called as "space of flows"[6].

- There is a continuous comparison between Individualism and communalism. Individuals survive in the network which maximizes sociability as individuals.

- In network society culture is dominated by media and Information products.

As discussed earlier the basic units of Network Society are the individual who are linked by networks. The extent of Network society is global and local .The components of society such as individuals and communities are no longer limited to time and space. The main basis of social units are shattered everywhere in network society as compared to traditional society. However, the individuals and communities choose their own contacts. Using telecommunication and Social media networks people maintain extremely high degree of connectivity .In a Network Society, face-to-face communication are also replaced by mediated communication. Interactions are done through instant messaging, virtual teams and chat groups.

Besides Castells, **Jan Van Dijk (2006)**[7] also discussed the features of Network Society:

• The main base of network society is science and rational thinking.

• The most important feature of network society is dynamic labour market formed by higher education.

• Informational items and other forms of electronic media influences culture in network society.

In sum, the contemporary society has its basis in Social networks. In the network society Social networking sites give importance to online interactions .These networking sites leads to interaction between individuals globally and virtually, transforming various aspects of daily life. The introduction of network society marks the emergence of social structure which is globally interdependent. Therefore, it is also marked by the emergence of network of cultures which are interacting and integrated with the common use of sharing. The network society is said to be the conclusion of technological expansion of industrial society which is unified with the process of westernization. Castells argues that globalization resulted in the creation of Network societies. In his work *the rise of network society (2010)* he argued that in the network society all the aspects of human life are dominated by networks. People are connected through *nodes*. Network society is different from other types of society. Networks are stretched to both national and cultural boundaries. It can be said that network society is one aspect of globalization. In the era of Network society, there are lesser boundaries and countries or organizations are interconnected and interlinked with each other. However, Castells also opines that the ultimate transformation of Communication, especially in the field of internet acts as the driving force behind the process of Globalization and the evolution of Network society. There are multiple ways to access internet. The data which is present on the internet can be accessed anywhere. In the era of Network Society, there is a revolutionary change in the space where communication happens and also witnesses the change in the form of media. Castells focused on three major changes in the media:

- That mass communication is mainly under the influence of international media .Radio, televison and Print media are some examples

- That people are now diverting towards personalized and tailor-made media contents. And in network society communicational channels are digitalized and interactive.

- That due to the new technology mass communication functions according to its own rules.Podcasts are individually provided contents which can be accessed anytime by anyone.

Castells believes that 3 procedures which is responsible for the development of this new system

- Restructuring of industrial economies to allow free trade flow.

- Freedom oriented cultural movements such as feminism and environmental movements.

- The ICT revolution.

Thus a Network Society is closely linked with Globalisation and role of Electronic Communication technologies which are responsible for the creation of new kinds of social structure in the late 20th century. The economic reconstruction resulted in weakening of the nation states and opening of open market development paradigm leading to social inclusion and exclusion between and with countries .The next section throws light on inclusion and exclusion in a network society.[8]

2.2(a) Inclusion and exclusion in Network Society

In the Network Society the societies are affected by inclusion and exclusion from the global networks. Castells argues that in network society exclusion is a built-in phenomenon now. The main basis of Network Society is networks. Networks only include those people and resources that are valuable to them and which assist them in fulfilling their tasks and exclude those resources that have no value to them. The other divide in the network society is the division of labor i.e., the people who are the source of innovation to the network society are included in the society. Those people and resources that are irrelevant as workers are excluded from the networks.

2.2(b) Power and empowerment in the Network society

Power is an important element in the field of social change. Power is termed as the ability to impose ones will on the other people. But in relation to Network Society the chief form of power is the control over communication. Some social groups' have access to the networks which makes easy for them to impose their values and goals on society at large. In the era of Network Society, Globalisation enables the people to make social, economic and political relationships which are not bounded by geographic location. People can communicate to each other with the help of mass media, phone, emails and fax .According to Castells; empowerment is strengthened by the social media networks in which social movements are connected through the internet. Social media promotes cultural diversity, innovations and a new kind of freedoms. Since the evolution of life as well as networking is a crucial part of people's life. The evolution of Network Society from traditional society also leads to changes in the relationships of its parts. This different structure of society also witnesses the transformation between abstract relations and concrete ties. Various trends that take place in the network society are:-

- The social units such as individuals, groups and organizations are linked to each other directly even at large distances. The increase in the connectivity in the network society has social and technological reasons both. The social reason is the increase in the social relations in modern society. The technological reasons can be the humongous rise in the mass media and improvement in transport and information and technology. As a result, there are more direct relations and a world which is much more connected.

- The integration of social and media networks leads to a change in infrastructure of society. Consequently; the public sphere will soon be a mosaic of spheres of similar denominators.

- Media is used to communicate and inform the society .This has made the people believe that social relationships are also associated with risks. Social and media networks are becoming social environments themselves. They discuss their own roles and circulate information among themselves. This has led to the relations of communications become self-referential.

- The media in the Network society represent the views and interest partially. They represent the information according to the needs of the audiences and the stakeholders.

- There is great degree of interaction amongst the social relations. People are more interactive now.

- In bureaucratic organizations, the use of networks is reducing complexity.[9]

There is sense of insecurity. The use of media networks makes the societal relations vulnerable. People are completely dependent on the media technologies which make the society the risk society. There is sense of insecurity. The use of media networks makes the societal relations vulnerable. People are completely dependent on the media technologies which make the society the risk society.Apart from these, some other new opportunities emerging after the evolution of Network Society are:

- Power lies with the people- People in the Network Society are empowered through SNSs.People can share real time information, search for job opportunities.

- Access to instant information- People can easily watch the episode of a serial on Netflix/Amazon prime and on others sites.

- Shift to digital values- The financial sector has witnessed immense transformation from a currency note to Bitcoin, credit card and to loyalty points.

- Economy is more collaborated- Businesses are now based on more collaborated models. Property owners and travellers can look up to properties and hotels through Airbnb.

- Blurring of boundaries- The boundaries that were earlier defined globally are now blurring away. People, communities and countries are connected to each globally.

The guiding principle in the age of Network Society is people live in an atmosphere of sharing .This is fundamentally changing the way people live, engage and collaborate. The main feature of contemporary society is the presence of Social networks, technical networks and Media networks. Social media focuses on the interaction which happens online .This facilitates its users to interact globally and virtually across the globe. The changes occurring majorly in social structure, culture and social behavior: networking as a prevalent organizational form: individuation as the main orientation of social behavior: and the culture of autonomy as the culture of the network society[10]. This expansion of the internet resulted in a shift towards reconstruction of social relationships and cultural changes in a society. The next section deals with the culture and the rise of a new subculture as a result of excessive use of social media.

2.3   Culture and Subculture: Concept and theoretical perspectives

The word 'culture' is an English word which is derived from the Latin term 'cult' or 'cultus' which means cultivating something or worshiping. In other words it means cultivating something or worshiping it to that extent so that its end product evolves as something admiring or respectful. It is a way of life i.e., the food a person eats, the clothes people wear, the language spoken by people and the god people worship are all counted in the aspects of culture. It is all the things that people inherit being the members of the society. Customs, traditions, festivals, one perspective on various issues of life are all included in cultures. It varies from place to place or from country to country. People are identified by their distinctive cultural traditions. It basically has two different components namely a)Material Culture- Consists of items that are related to the material things. Examples:-food, clothing etc.)Non-material culture- It refers to ideas, thoughts, and belief etc. Culture thus can be denoted as a man-made environment including all the material and non-material components which are transmitted from one generation to another in the form of culture, literature and other recreational and enjoyment patterns. It is only the culture that makes a person ethical and teaches a person the values of peace, tolerance and love.

2.3 (a) Culture

There are numerous definitions of culture, and it influences every single act of the people in the society due to ideas, attitudes, behaviors and their values. It is something which is not inherited genetically but is common to all the members of the society. Culture is used in various senses. Tylor was the first person to use the word culture .He in his book named *Primitive culture* (1871)[11] explained culture as that complex whole which includes knowledge, belief, art, law, customs acquired by man as a member of society. The sum of this is culture is that social tradition which is given by society to its members. Therefore it is the innovation of man for fulfilling the social needs. Socialization is the process through which it is transferred from one generation to another. According to R.H. Lowie[12], culture is the sum total of social .Therefore,

Culture is mainly the way of life of a group in a society; it is particular patterns of behavior. It is dynamic in nature .It keeps changing in different .It changes according to time. Thus, Culture is a whole of elements, traits or parts, way of life of a particular segment of a society. Culture is something which is constructed socially and shared by the members of the society. Any society can never exist apart from culture. A society is always, and of groups which carry and transmit culture. It is culture which helps in distinguishing individual from individual and group from group. Society cannot operate without cultural directives. It is that collective heritage which is learned by individuals and passed from one generation to another generation. The person learns culture and in turn, may reshape the culture and bring changes which become part of the heritage of the coming generations.

TYPES OF CULTURE

The different types of culture identified by anthropologists and sociologists are:

- *High Culture*: It is usually referred to as the cultural traits of high status. The art forms which were established long before are the examples of high cultures. Some examples are-operas, paintings such as Leonardo da Vinci, elite goods, high fashion, maintaining an i-phone, wearing branded clothes etc. Some communities are more civilized than others; some people are more cultured than others.

- *Folk Culture:* It is referred to as that cultures of ordinary people specially those who are living in pre-industrial societies. It arises from the grass roots and reflects directly the encounters of the people. For e.g.:-traditional folk songs, classical stories of the local people etc. It is something which is trustworthy and not artificially created.

- *Mass Culture:* It is the culture of modern society or industrial society. It is a consequence of mass media such as films, daily soaps, music, and social media. It is something which is broadcasted and distributed to individuals rather than arising from day-to-day interactions with each other. The different platforms of mass media are the main transmitters of culture. The television and internet broadcasts content that reflects acceptable and unacceptable behaviors. The format of certain content invites the viewers to laugh. Mass media acquires an important position in today's society. Modern methods of communication captivate the people through free flow of information and entertainment .It has the capability to shape people's consciousness by playing a democratic role in the society. It has the power to manipulate people's opinion. It also reflects social reality. The content available on mass media sources such as television, radio, internet and social media shapes the opinion of people and their lifestyle. However this is also debasing the culture of ordinary normal people and creating issues in today's society.

- *Popular Culture:* It is a kind of culture which is appreciated by large number of people. It is that kind of culture which is made by the people for themselves. The sale os a particular CD, book and attendance at certain concert is probably the best example of popular culture.

- *Global Culture:* It implies that that the people of the world are opting for one single culture that is affecting each and every part of the world. This denotes that due to the process of globalization certain aspects of culture are crossing the boundaries and are humongously accepted by the people of the world. The different cultures of the world are simply under the influence of western culture which is gradually increasing the hybridity in culture which involves amalgamation of various cultures which gives rise to a new culture. In modern society, people migrate from one place to another in search of jobs and education .This migration led to the mixing of cultures .Globalization has already shrunken the world. The advent of internet led to interchange of ideas .It allows a person sitting in India and access a library of any university of U.K...As globalization involves free flow of economy and knowledge. Global culture has succeeded to bring one homogenous culture in the world.

- *Subculture*: It is a culture which is common to a group of people that have something in common with each other (they share a problem, an interest, a practice) which distinguishes them in a significant way from other social groups.

2.3(b) Subculture:

It is that social group within a group with lifestyle that is different from the culture of the group as a whole. The main examples of youth subculture can be Goths, punks, moshers', hippies etc. The members of these groups have different taste of dressing, music and lifestyle .But they are not totally different from the other members of the society. People choose on their own whether to belong to specific youth culture. The important source of social identity can be subcultures. The internet and social media is nowadays an important instrument of change in the lives of people. There is no doubt that new technology is significantly impacting the culture .The rapid advancements in the digital technology brought netizens closer together .Social media facilitates the interaction between people of different cultures. It is emerging as a platform for the easy exchange of ideas, cultural values and views. Today in people's life what matters the most is their picture on their social media account. It provides communication platform for the people to communicate with close friends and strangers (by liking pictures, status updates, wall updates etc.). This technology is used in a very profound way by social and political movements to promote their cause. The culture of everyday life is now extremely intertwining with the Social media. The introduction of online dating sites is changing the way people construct their significant relationships. Social networking sites such as Facebook, Twitter and Instagram helps in bringing the people together with different background and cultures and hence responsible for bringing about a new culture. The growing importance of virtual world is impacting the way men and women conduct their everyday affairs. It has become so prominent in the modern world because it is convenient and efficient to communicate with the people around the world. The joining of the virtual with the real is the reality of the contemporary culture. The impact of internet especially Social media has significantly transformed the lives of the youth.

Characteristics of subculture

There is no perfect definition of Subculture by sociologists. It can better be understood by the characteristics of Subculture.

- *Diffuse networks:* Subcultures do not involve a formal leadership, well defined organizational structure and formal membership. It consists of membership which is loose and informal. Sub culturists can be easily being identified as part of a subculture and at the same time they can interact with the other people in different social and cultural networks. As a result, the boundaries of both mainstream culture and subculture are indistinguishable as both can have common ideas and also coincide in individuals lives. In other words, both culture and subculture interact and adapt with each because exchange of meanings and values are also done.

- *Share similar values:* Sub culturists have similar values, believe, and practices. As a particular subculture emerges unique meaning is formed to define a distinct practices and cultural objects as well as to differentiate it from mainstream culture. These meanings continuously grow and create new meanings. Actually meanings are both created and learned through social interactions which are totally different from the mainstream culture of the society.

- *Shared identity:* The most important distinguisher between subculture and simple social group is a collective form of self-identification. Sub culturists have an innate sense of connection and relationship with the other members of their subculture. Subculture consists of people who share a strong common identity. This connection helps them to bond over and refer each other as "family".

- *Resistance:* Resistance either passive or active to hegemonic cultural values often leads to emergence of subcultural groups. It is dependent on participant's motive to resist.

- *Marginalization:* The people of subculture consists of people who have excluded thinking and have the opinion that they do not fit well in the mainstream culture. Since these people cannot meet the norms and values of the normal social group culture. Consequently, the participants of Subculture often become stigmatized by mainstream culture society culture.

- *Stratification, values and specialized vocabulary:* As dominant cultures have different stratification system subcultures too have stratification systems. However, the stratification system in subculture is constantly changing the collective values within the group. Another feature that helps to differentiate between the participants of subculture and the people of mainstream culture are few words and phrases that are only understood by the people of subculture. It also illustrates the intensity of their involvement in the subculture

2.3(c) Theories of Culture and Subculture

Functionalist perspective on culture

The functionalists believe that all the parts of the society function together in order to form society as a whole. They imply sense of norms, values and lifestyles. Cultural values guides people in making their choices. They view culture in terms of evolutionary perspectives. They focus on the changing nature of culture. Durkheim and Mauss developed a theory about the origin of human culture.

Marxist theory of culture

Conflict theorists argue that social structure is a based on unequal distribution of power which creates differences between class, race gender and age. For them culture is nothing but a supporting system of privileged group .In male dominated society women strive for equality. Cultures value systems also consist of inequalities. The cultural norms of society benefit some people but hurt others. The main idea of conflict theory is impact of people who owns the means of economic production on the people who sell their labor .While in contemporary society's rich nations having expertise in technology versus nations which are lagging behind in technology and education sector. People or nations having less power as compared to rich nations has inability to cope up with cultural change.

Marx in his famous work *the German ideology (1846)*[13],

The ideas of the ruling class in every age, the ruling ideas: i.e., the class which is dominant material force in society is at the same time its dominant intellectual force. The class which has the means of material production at its disposal has control at the same time over the means of mental production, so that in consequence the ideas of those that lack the means of mental production are, in general subject to it. The dominant ideas are nothing more than the ideal expression of the dominant material relationships grasped as ideas.

In contemporary society, the power is vested with the mass media (television, radio, internet).They transmit the ideas of the ruling class through these platforms. They depict the cultural industry in terms of their economic benefit. Commercial media organizers act according to the need of advertisers produces sex and violent content. And those media organization whose revenue are controlled by political parties or state show the content which is in favor of them. Thus the main structure of media is controlled by the ruling class of any society. And soon it becomes a culture.

Interactionist perspective on Culture

It is a sociological perspective that sees face-to-face interaction between the members of the society. They argue that culture is formed because of the interaction between the people interact and also because people interpret others actions. Symbolic interactionists argue that individuals derive meaning from both objects in the environment and actions of others and believes that human interaction is a continues process. Language is the best means for a person to communicate the meanings derived from the object and action. The proponents believes that culture as highly dynamic in nature because it keeps changing the meaning that is interpreted and also the ways it is interacted when they convey meanings.

Neo-Marxist theory of culture

Neo Marxists assumed that that there is no connection between class and culture and it is totally free from economic influence. They denied the fact that economic factors determine culture in a straight forward way. In this context, Williams argues that:

A Marxist theory of culture will recognize diversity and complexity, will take account
of continuity within change, will allow for chance and certain limited autonomies,
but, with these reservations, will take the facts of the economic structure and the
consequent social relations as the guiding string on which a culture is
woven[14].(William,1961)

Williams work was more historical and creative than any other Marxists work. He argued that the Marxists work had narrow focus about art and; literature. They focused on the fact that all the aspects of social reality influence culture. Therefore he assumed that culture is way of life i.e., a social process and hence it should be used logically.

THEORIES OF SUBCULTURE

Marxist new sub cultural theories

Marxists argue that societies evolve when people get together in order to earn living. The forces of production are responsible to shape social relationships. In Marxists theory, the most important social group in any capitalist societies is class. Class is determined by the person having relationships with the ownership of property. The class which has ownership of property are-bourgeoisie and the working class – proletariat. These classes are all the time in conflict with each other. Those who own the means of production exploit them who work for them. Eventually the working start realizing that they are being exploited and decide to overthrow capitalism and to create communist society. In a communist kind of society, means of production will be owned communally. The proletariats have their own culture which includes their dressing sense, food, lifestyle etc. which are included under subculture. This constant competition between both the classes leads to conflict between them. This brings change in the society.

Post sub cultural thought

Various theorists of post subcultural thought are of the opinion that subcultures are different from the mainstream culture. They argue that there is a diffusion of culture through the process of globalization and also because there is interconnectedness of people, thoughts, ideas and this has changed the way subculture emerges. In the era of Globalization consumerisms is also responsible to for the emergence of subcultural communities by making subcultural habits such as online shopping, posting pictures on Social media, buying branded clothes and products that are available for anyone to buy. There is an increasing interconnectedness between people . Individuals now are free to follow any subcultural group identity. Therefore, Post subcultural theorists believes that the process of globalization and mixing or amalgamation of cultures allows people to choose which subculture they want to embody.

Micro-celebrities

Micro celebrity phenomenon views the people who influence the viewers of Social media sees the audience as a fan base and maintains their popularity by managing them. This practice helps in constructing the presentation of the self with the consumption of these images by the viewers in mind. Micro celebrity is a visual selfie presentation strategy which is done to raise economy because more likes and views means more success for the artist. This theory is especially relevant to the "Snapchatfam" practice where emojis are and filters are used by the followers which improves the online status of the influencer.

Phatic communication

Phatic communication focuses on the ways that how interaction over the social media platform favors on their limited availability and attention. "connection over content". It tells the others users know that "one is still there" by the use of Social media. It constructs a connected presence. The connected presence plays an important role as keeping in touch is more important than the information is transferred.

2.4 SUBCULTURE AND SOCIAL MEDIA: AN INTERFACE

Since Social Media has been integrated into the daily lives of the increasing number of people. There is a vast impact of it on the activities, social relationships and worldviews of the younger generation. It is tremendously shaping their values, believes and their social behavior patterns. Internet or Social media acts as an innovation force that has an intense influence on the youth. Various other terms is used to describe the youth of this generation such as Net generation, millennium generation and digital natives[10]. These tags denote a large group of people especially who grew up in the period which witness the expansion of internet and the environment which is totally media –rich using the devices such as computers, laptop, Mobile phones etc. which helps them in constantly connecting them with their friends and relatives through these electronic devices. In network society these sites are used for social interaction, online shopping, dating and online gaming. In current society, the youth's cultural consumption includes various cultural products like TV, laptops and Mobile phones. However by utilizing these spaces users especially youth is gradually becoming empowered. Users are able to overcome the geographical limitations by reaching out to people with similar likes. Through their innovation presentations on the internet they act as co-producers for the large and global audiences. Online activity is somewhat different from ones offline activities. Thus, youth using an online communication method maybe geographically apart (experiences distinct hours at different locations) but share common interests, identical set of activities . By using this virtual space, they express their real or inner selves because of the anonymity of the internet. People use internet to do old things in new ways. The advent of Web 2.0 increases the active participation of users. People are the passive consumers of the content and information online. The online experience of doing certain activities are changing now which is leading to bring cultural changes or the emergence of new subculture amongst the youth.

List of subcultures emerging through Social media.

Replacement of offline markets by online markets

From the main street to the Wall Street, from the school classroom to the board rooms there is a kind of revolution happening after the advent of Social media. There is a fundamental shift in ways we communicate. Social media has touched almost every aspect of people life. As its use is increasing in people's lives, the opportunities to grow are day by day is also increasing at a faster rate. In the digital era, the business is also dependent on the Social media profile. Social networking sites such as Instagram and Facebook are used by brands to advertise their products. Online worlds of Social world and e-commerce are merging in different ways.

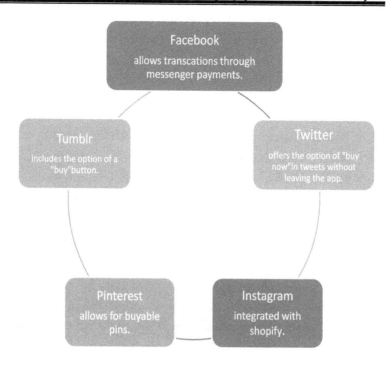

Each Social media platform offers various features/options to sell goods and services. Brands such as Craftsvilla work through Facebook and Instagram and have millions of customers. Women nowadays prefer working from home. They advertise any product on their Facebook account and sell it. This is changed the way people earn money, do business and shop.

Online groups and communities

Social networking sites such as Facebook, Twitter and WhatsApp facilitate its members the opportunity to create and join groups of people online. Groups are formed on the basis of family, former classmates, interests of hobbies, causes, religious and jobs. The membership in these groups is totally voluntary by the approval of group administrator. Twitter facilitates hashtag communities. It is a group of people who use a particular keyword after a number of hashtag (#) in their tweets. Its participation is voluntary and revolves around a common interest. All publicly used hashtags are visible to the world. This has changed the classic definition of groups. The main function of Social groups is the advancement of conversation and connection among the members. As these groups are not visible to anyone it is comfortable for its members to express themselves. With the use of Social media groups one can stay in touch with the friends, family members and colleagues irrespective of the time and distance. This has brought the world closer to each other.

Snapchat effect

Snapchat is the amongst the most popular Social media applications used by the youth. Its impact has grown rapidly. It facilitates its members by providing a medium for pictures/photos and selfies to be disseminated. Selfies are embedded with text, filters (especially of a dog, zebra, tiger, cowman etc.) and doodles .In this context, Dana Boyd argues how youngsters use Snapchat to share photos and videos which automatically disappear after 10 seconds "inside jokes, silly pictures and images that were funny only in the moment[11]". These are used to communicate with friends as well as with family members as a funnier alternative to simple messaging on WhatsApp and other SNSs. New features are included time to time to maintain the interest of its users .It enables the users to robe them in masks and feathers, or can also change themselves into animals .It provides opportunity for creativity. It could be an innocent a great way to connect with the friends. But it also has its effect on the mental health of its participants. It can lead to various negative issues such as anxiety, loneliness and body shaming. Platforms like Snapchat and Instagram focuses on pictures which can be difficult for its participants to deal with the self-esteem. People might think that their bodies aren't good enough. It can also lead to eating disorders, fear of missing out and bullying. It is mostly used by the people of young age group and it leads to low self-esteem. In some way it facilitates the best and the worst of youth's culture.

Conspicuous Consumption

The theory of conspicuous consumption was developed by Veblen. It defines the lavish spending on goods and services by the people in order to display/flaunt their status. In the digital era, people demonstrate their social status on Social media. This has become giant game of the Internet today. On the Social networking Sites a person can portray how influential and interesting he/she is. People posts on their Facebook profile that they are eating in a five-star restaurant but in reality, they are not doing so. In order to maintain their social status, they do anything and everything. People post their photos while standing in a mall near a branded showroom irrespective of the fact whether they shop or not. Just to show their friends that they are leave a lavish lifestyle they can go to any extent. But this is eventually creating a feeling of jealousy and low self-esteem amongst the youth.

Self-presentation

Self-presentation is a process through which individuals create their identity. In the era of Social media, it is best and most used platform. Social networking sites facilitate its users to create a profile and to upload and share photos, videos and personal details. People posts information on their account in such a way that it looks attractive to the other users. All these social media platforms encourage the use of pictures in online profiles. That is why people pay special attention to clicking pictures so that they can post it online on their profiles. There are certain application which promoting editing the pictures by applying filters which include hiding the spots from the face, sliming the face and making it look attractive. But this is encouraging the people to hide their real features from the world. One thing that online profile pictures are leading to is instead of experiencing the life from the own perspective or point of view, people view the world from the perspective of how others will view. Image on Social media is known as online image or Social avatar, shows that life of its users but in certain cases it is dissociated from it. Certain sites like Twitter which facilitates interaction with the strangers. Discrepancies between real personality and online personality is found which leads to mental distress, psychological compartmentalization of the personality and increasing comparisons with others exaggerated lifestyles and measures of popularity. The upward social comparison will lead to feeling of dejection; however the downward social comparison would most likely lead to positive feeling and increasing self -esteem. People post the most socially desirable segment of their lives to create their ideal representation. Eventually, people are devoting much of their time on Social media and it can lead to drastic consequences in their life.

Dating sites

After the emergence of Social media all the aspects of a person life has totally changed. Among all the other aspects online dating has already become popular. Sites such as *Facebook, Instagram* and *Twitter* also recommend users with pictures of nearby people. The app called *Tinder* allows its users to *'like'* or *'dislike'* the picture. And if two users like each other than a *'match'* is made. They can interact with each other. This has changed the whole definition of dating. Tinder aims to match on the basis of locality rather than interests. The people are looking for love or lust relationships breaking down boundaries even for long-term relationships. In earlier times marriages were fixed by the parents and relatives. There were even times when relationships started with handshake or a smile, rather than a click, like or a swipe. Online dating is successful in removing the traditional obstacles such as time and space. But some people are unaware of the fact that all the members are not there to find true love some of them are also there for sexual encounters. This is changing the fabric of society.

Memes Culture

The internet is the most complex media till now. Although it provides everything that the previous media did but there is something special about it. Social networking sites is the most used platform. It conveys everything to everyone and it the biggest tool of development these days. Each and every social networking site is loaded with information for its users. One thing which is getting into limelight is the use memes. Memes is a replicator of something. It can be a catchy tune, picture or a video. There is nothing new in the concept of memes. It is a fundamental unit of transmission of communication and culture on the Social media. Before the advent of Social media cultural transmissions was done through rhymes, jokes and quotes. But after the introduction of Social media, large number of memes are made consisting of quotes, funny thoughts, motivational thoughts, political images, images about love and care etc. These are most popular on Facebook and Twitter and it can be shared on various other platforms such as WhatsApp, Instagram and Snapchat etc. Many users share Memes in order to establish stronger connection online where face-to-face contact is limited. It makes the person look intelligent, trendy and funny. There are memes in which there is written that "if you love a particular person than tag so and so person in order to show them your love". People may find it a good platform to express themselves out of happiness, sadness, shock, nostalgia and fear. But it generates positive emotions rather than negative. Even Facebook has entered into the age of Meme.

New criminal tendencies

The primary use of Social networking sites isinstant communication or interaction with the friends and other people. But its use is increasing day-by-day it is also sometimes used for harassing, threatening and unwelcomed communication. The people who commit crime through Social networking Sites are called as Cyber criminals. They take out personal details of the users such as name, profile pictures, phone number, email address and use it dangerously. Earlier bullying was done in the school but in recent times children and youngsters are bullied online. Cyber bullies hide their identity. Internet is available at a cheaper price for the people. It is easily accessible to everyone. People create fake profile and hide their identity and talk to people. Dating sites like Tinder, being anonymous is a secure feeling which encourages person to commit crime in the virtual world rather than a real world. Social networking sites is not only attractive but also a biggest source of cyber crime and through which new criminal tendencies are emerging.

Social media is making people lonelier

Although Social media makes the people connected to others. But there are speculations that it makes the people feel lonelier. People are busy engaging in their devices and social media platforms. And missing the actual experiences of life that is actually happening around them. People are spending time virtually together but in reality, alone. People who have low self esteem could very easily look at photos posted by friends and find themselves wanting. Sometimes they even feel rejected when they update a status and no one *likes* it or *comment* on it. People use Social media as a substitute of face-to-face social relation especially those who have social anxiety. They have a fear in talking to people. But when they go online they feel connected with the other people because they don't have to face them in real life. Hence Social media is not so social.

Youth have better choice of self-socialization

Earlier the socialization was done through parents, school, peers and neighbourhood. But in the digital era, where internet is almost free of cost. And Social media is widely used by the youth. It is also a source of socialization. There can be five uses of Social media by the youth which can also be counted under the heading of Socialization.

Entertainment-Social media facilitates its users to share videos and photos,check in location,make online purchases,use different applications and play games.It has a great entertainment value for its users.

Identity formation-The users circulate the information that potryas their potential and qualities and what they want other users to know.

High sensation-There are various things on Social media that inspires its users and changed their lifestyle to an extent.

Youth culture identification-Social media consumption gives a sense of being connected to a larger network through which they are united certain specific values and interests.

This is a common theme of uses of Social media .The users draw material from the social networking sites that contribute to their socialization. When they seek these uses from Social media they participate in a media-based youth subculture which is a part of their socialization. Due to the availability of several things on Social media users have a choice of what best suits to them .It allows the users to engage themselves in the process of self-socialization as they are able to select the media products that are most attractive to them.

New sources of leisure and entertainment

Youth spent most of their leisure time in front of television and computer screens. As the use of Social media increases rapidly, it caused a change in their leisure behavior. Once a person opens his social media profile it is overloaded with the news feed containing pictures, videos, and news material. Earlier, people used to pass time with their friends whereas now in the digital era one can connect with the friend who is 800 miles away from him/her. It is not necessary for a person to go out and meet a friend it can also be done just by staying at home. They are accessible and maybe socially connected from home. They call it a form of bonding with each other. Unlike watching movie, users play online game whether alone or with the friends or family members. People create their videos sometimes of their own. It emerges like a trend for eg. The Kiki Challenge which became a trend on the Instagram which involves jumping out of a moving car to break into a dance. The advancement of digital devices increases the variety of leisure activities amongst the youth.

Virtual Empathy

In real life empathy means to understand the feelings and emotions of other people. Virtual empathy means to understand the feelings of another person through the virtual medium. In the world of Social media everyone is a friend of each other whether they are known to each other or not. People are comfortable in accepting the friend request from the people who are friends of their friends. In this digital era, some common ways of virtual empathy are: -

Thumbs up: The simplest way of expressing virtual empathy is through a "like". People on Social media re being "liked "across borders. Liking somebody posts or picture on Social media is a way of expressing understanding, supporting, solidarity and approval. More likes on posts more support. Sometimes it is biggest reason of depression.

Sharing and commenting: Commenting a kind of virtual empathy which requires deeper amount of understanding. When a comment is done on a post it is given more weightage than likes. Sharing is done in order to support something. For eg.an event or an announcement.

Going live: Social networking sites such as Facebook, Instagram and Twitter now have a feature of going live. Through this a person can experience everything without having met the particular person. It is highly advanced and more powerful feature.

Selfie

According to Oxford Dictionaries the year 2013 marks the introduction of the word 'selfie'. It refers to the art of taking a self-picture through camera and sharing it on Social media. Posting selfies on Social media have become common with the advent of ICTs .It is an effective tool of self-potrayal. Selfie is an important part in today's society. The specific nature of Social media is self-representations and the process of sharing selfies on online platform has developed over the years. Both celebrities and non-celebrities post selfie on social media which is somehow leading to the emergence of selfie culture. The basic aim behind taking a selfie is to say 'look at me' in a public sphere with the main motive is to get attention. Instagram plays an humongous role in promoting selfie because it is solely pictures based unlike other networks such as Facebook. Although it is just like Facebook people update their post on it. It is surprising to note that while taking selfie some people also died. Death is worst affect that occurred besides that people also suffer from anxiety, inferiority complex and jealousy. People are fond of taking selfie and post them on their Social media account .Further they keenly wait for *likes* and *comments* .The 'American psychiatric association 'has for perfection. However the positive aspect of taking selfie is that it uplifts someone's self-esteem.

Self-esteem levels

Self-esteem is referred to as overall evaluation of oneself be it as positive or negative. Social media facilitates its users with less self-confidence to interact interpersonally and involve in public behaviors with the reduced risk of social anxiety. There can be many reasons to use Social media such as to keep updated, to seek information, entertainment and communication with others. People find best social media outlets that fulfill their desires. It is observed that women tend to take more selfies than men.

Impact of Selfies on Self-confidence levels

Selfie is a kind of double-sided coin. For some users it is a self esteem booster and for others it is something that makes them awful about their looks and their lives. Many users especially teenagers spend lots and lots of money and time to look attractive and which boots their self -esteem.

Narcissism and Social networking sites

Narcissism is a belief that one self is superior over others. They constantly seek admiration from other. Sites such as Facebook and Twitter facilitates its users to participate in attention-seeking behaviours. Narcissits believe that all their followers and social networking friends are genuinely interested in knowing what they are doing so it is important for them to share their experiences. Narcissistic individuals tend to keep focus of their profile's content specifically on themselves.

Effects of Selfies on Socio-psychological characteristics of people

The addiction of taking selfies is linked to narcissism, self-obsession, isolation, and even suicide. Social networking Sites such as Instagram and Snapchat which are totally image based, forces its users to post a beautiful image. These pictures or posts are often the first impressions people put out on their Social media profiles to attract friends, romantic interests and other people.

Skin damage

Taking selfie continuously exposes the face to light and radiation of the phone which damages the skin. It ultimately promotes wrinkles on screen and speed up aging. Experts' advice that DNA streaks breaks down from the electromagnetic radiation coming from the mobile phones which places oxidative stress on cells .It damages the skin.

Lowers self-confidence

Almost all the people post their photographs online to seek attention and approval in the form of 'likes'. This particular behavior could lead to mental health problems. Not getting the number of likes expected will only make them nervous and lowers their self-confidence. This also affects their thoughts. There are lots of people who post their photos on Social media in the hope of likes and comments but due to this they are also making themselves vulnerable and to negative comments and cyber bullying .Especially teens see it as an embarrassment when on their birthday they do not receive large number of post on their profile. People use various beauty apps so that they can beautify their photo to look good on their profile. This promotes materialism in the social world.

Suicide

Researchers argue that selfie addiction leads to suicuide. Experts are of the view that taking more than 10 selfies a day can lead to dysmorphic disorder .People are totally unaware about the threats associated with electronic gadgets and social media .People waste their time while taking selfie in order to look good they also undergo various surgeries which somehow harms their health.

Mental illness

Excessive selfie taking is detrimental for a person's mental health and leads to indulgence in narcissm, lowself-esteem and attention seeking behavior .People are constantly attached to the mobile screens without even setting limits for using it. Selfies raise the risk of narcissm. However, it is discovered that interacting with other types of social media is linked to depression and low self-esteem.

Damages real relationships

Excessive selfie taking can damage friendship and relationship. It negatively impacts their level of intimacy.

Plastic surgery

When people take selfie and feel that their appearance is not good .This leads to opt for plastic surgery .People often feel disappointed when they feel that their picture is not up to date .Users use filters to beautify their images. The most drastic option is going for plastic surgery and other cosmetic treatments.

Social comparison

In the era of Social media, it is easy for people to compare their life with others .Social networking sites such as Facebook, Twitter and Instagram is the most common platform where people easily showcase themselves. People tend to compare their life with their online friend who sometimes makes them feel jealousy and low about themselves.

In this era, the internet and the technology influences peoples life directly. In this manner, the selfie affects the youth. Youngsters share their selfies on Facebook, WhatsApp, twitter, and onInstagram. The selfie brings negative impact on youth such as skin damage, loss of self-confidence and lowers self-esteem, damage real relationship, selfie deaths, and plastic surgery on youth. Youngsters should understand the positive and negative aspects of taking excessive Selfie.

Conclusion

The rise in Technological advancement has totally changed the society .It has also impacted the culture in various ways and led to the emergence of new Subculture amongst the youth. In this era of Internet there is a rising network structure of society. The important element of network society is Social media. It has changed people's lifestyle, language etc. The generation who uses social media is called millennial generation. A social networking site facilitates its users to maintain not only personal relationships, but also to idealize personalities. With the use of social media such as Facebook ,Instagram,Whatsapp and Twitter the main channel for social interaction, it is observed that many Millennial feel the need to portray themselves in ways that attract the attention of their peers. Thereby altering their values, lifestyle and behavior patterns, online communities are emerging which have altered the classic definition of groups, but also have been able to bring the world closer .Self presentation /identity has acquired a key role and all efforts are directed towards it. However, there is sometimes dissociation between the online self presentation and the real self. This can cause distress and even dejection. Online dating which is beyond time and space is changing the future of traditional society .Entertainment and leisure has a new face; computer screen and social media are the new destination for leisure. Online chatting, online gaming, newsreading are the new leisure time activities Shopping sites have brought the entire market at the doorsteps making consumption easy and accessible. A new subculture is emerging which has its roots in virtual transactions, based on shared interests and identical activities .However, the lack of physical proximity is creating lonely people walking on lonely crowds .They are missing the real experiences of life and engaging in virtual experiences .This anonymity in Social media is giving rise to new forms of criminal tendencies .Social media is thus bringing in a whole new culture which has its roots in virtual space but it is also affecting the youth the most. The current study will help in finding out whether a similar virtual culture is emerging amongst the youth of Jaipur city.

Notes and references

1. Global village-The world which is linked by telecommunication or information.

2. Castells, M. (2010).*The rise of Network Society*. United Kingdom, Blackwell publishing Ltd.

3. Nie, N.H. (2001).Sociability, interpersonal relation and the internet: Reconciling conflicting findings. *American Behavioral Scientists, 45.420*-435.

4. Dijk,J.(1999),*Network Society, Social aspects of New media* ,Sage:London.

5. Castells, M. (2004), *The Network Society: A Cross-Cultural Perspective*, MA: Elgar, Northhampton.

6. Castells, M. (2004), *The Network Society: A Cross-Cultural Perspective*, MA: Elgar, Northhampton.

7. Dyk, Jan van (2006).*The network Society,* Second edition, Sage, London.

8. Castells, M. (2004), *The Network Society: A Cross-Cultural Perspective*, MA: Elgar, Northhampton.

9. Castells, M. (2004), *The Network Society: A Cross-Cultural Perspective*, MA: Elgar, Northhampton.

10. https://www.bbvaopenmind.com/wp-content/uploads/2014/03/BBVA-OpenMind-Knowledge-Banking-for-a-Hyperconnected-Society-Francisco-Gonzalez.pdf.pdf

11. Tylor, E. (1871).*Primitive Culture.* London: Dover Publications Inc.

12. Lowie, R.H. (1920).*Primitive Society.* New York: Boni and Liveright

13. Marx, K. (1932).*The German Ideology.* New York: Prometheus Books.

14. Williams, R. (1961).*Culture and Society.* Penguin, Harmondsworth.

15. MarcPrensky, "Digital Natives, Digital Immigrants Part 1," *On the Horizon* 9.5 (October 2001): 1–6;Don Tapscott, *Growing Up Digital: The Rise of the Net Generation* (New York: McGraw Hill, 1998).

16. B,Danah.(2014).*Its Complicated:The Social lives of networked Teens.*New Haven CT:Yale University Press.

CHAPTER: 3

REVIEW OF LITERATURE

3.1 Introduction

A literature is a body of writings which consists of knowledge including findings such as theoretical and factual on a particular topic. Literature review refers to the critical review of that knowledge. They are secondary sources. One cannot conduct study without assessing and evaluating the available texts which is relevant to the area of study. The usage of Social media is increasing day-by-day. Many studies were conducted to study the impact of social networking sites on various aspects of society such as education, politics, and health, culture of the youth and inter-relationship. Review of literature on Impact of Social media is to explore what research has already been done in this area, the theoretical explanations analyzed to understand Social media and society. Besides all this, it is also worthwhile to analyze its impact on culture. As Social media is a topic of mass communication and culture is a topic of sociology so the books of mass communication and sociology were reviewed.

3.2 Studies on culture

Sulthana (2021)[1] opines that Covid-19 is the most disastrous pandemic in the world. People were advised to stay at home .Platforms such as uses Facebook, Twitter and Instagram etc .were used to access the information instantly .The biggest search engine Google was used to access the information on Covid-19 .It was analyzed that using Google search for accessing the information about Covid-19 increased in the period between 2019-2020. Internet usage was high at that time. Lockdown was one of the main reasons which increased the online shopping habit. The study concluded that the people were in the favors to continue to buy online as it is easy to get products at their door step .There are also other benefits of buying online such as discount coupons, cash back, discounts and easy return.

Joshi (2019)[2] argues that the two big problems millennial's face today are-loneliness despite being over-connected and indecisiveness due to the infinite options. In cities like Mumbai, Delhi and Bengaluru people use an offline social network called BeatMap because it has helped them to overcome this problem. It is a new initiative which invites people to attend and host parties with strangers and bond with them on music, movies and stand-up comedy. In the digital age of Social media people prefer to connect over Social networks but they end up being lonely and full of anxiety. This new application or initiative is giving rise to a new culture.

Jalal (2018)[3] argues that culture is the social practice ,behavior ,food habits and lifestyle patterns of a society which changes over a time. Globalization is also responsible for bringing changes the culture. After the emergence of globalization, the western culture became prominent in India and the culture of India is transmitted to the rest of the world. The cultural practices of the older generation is replaced by the western cultures .Earlier people used to live together, celebrate festivals ,less restaurant culture was there but now it is now replaced by the western culture. The advent of Globalization has provided people to fulfill their demand at anytime or anywhere .However, the author also opined that Globalization also prepared the people to work in multi-cultural world which enables them to think creatively and also helps them to realize the global responsibilities of the global world.

Kwan (2018)[4] opines that creativity is bounded by culture and individuals of different cultures take creativity differently .Cultural values lessens innovation outputs. Certain types of values such as power distance, uncertainty avoidance and cultural tightness discourages the person from choosing unique ideas. The author argues that innovation can transform the culture by altering the material condition in any society. Kwan concludes that creativity, innovation and culture are linked. But culture is understood differently across the world.

Bhoje (2015)[5] argues that culture includes the beliefs,objects,values and other characteristics common to the members of the group or society. It comprises many societal values such as language, customs, values, norms, organization and institutions. The culture of India is unique because of its diversity. There is hardly any culture in the world which is as varied as India has. After globalization it has left its footprints everywhere the interchange of world views and ideas resulted in a major transformation of the lifestyle of people. The youth do not believe in traditional aspect and the culture is not traditional anymore .The author concluded that many Indian traditions and festivals are centuries old and have an important place in Indian culture. The internet is also playing a huge role in preserving these traditions in the global space.

Domirani(2014)[6] conducted a research on the cultural impact of globalization on the national media of broadcasting in Iran and concluded that education and lifestyle were getting influenced by the transnational corporations owned media in the age of globalization. The author argues that globalization impacts society and transforms their religious, cultural and political views .He suggested that media and educational institutions should also transform according to the challenges of globalization.

Narasimhamurthy(2014)[7] opines that individuals values, behaviors and beliefs are shaped by culture. It is a way of life which is passed from one generation to the other. But there are millions of other culture in the world with its own unique identity and nature .However in the twentieth century, the culture arises from a new form of communication technology .The advent of new communication technology has linked the world together and makes it easy for the people to communicate and interact with people and culture around the world. The invent of Social networking Sites has become important part of people daily lives. Social media promotes interconnectedness and interdependence culturally diverse world. It facilitates the people to access the information that is available on the internet. The author argued that internet has resulted in the advancement and homogenization of the culture across the world. This is because of its ability to access information about other cultures. The exposure of Social media led to the spread of cultural elements. The author concludes that this new form of communication technology have successfully connected people and brings people of various cultures together which is responsible in the emergence of global culture .

Ghosh(2011)[8] argues that humungous changes have occurred in the economy, society and culture due to the globalization of market, network and relation in the contemporary world. The emergence of global society also generates challenges in the traditional structures of the east societies. Societies depend on their history, social structure and cultural features to globalize. The author opines that globalization in the contemporary society is characterized by economy that is dominated by services. The major force of social change in contemporary society is consumption rather than production.Todays society is a place in which everything is for sale. Culture in contemporary world, is shaped in a way that it attaches to the controls of market and utilized customs, practices and rituals to its benefits. The author also talks in Indian context, the huge impact of electronic media have also impacted the society and also leads to change in the traditional modes of the cultural expression, relations and language at regional and national levels. The author concludes that there is homogenization of culture due to globalization. However he also argues that globalization in India is also multifaceted, and complex. There is a spread of plural cultural elements across the globe. The author identifies Globalization as a means to construct new identities but the challenge is to recognize and respect the globalized social life.

3.3 Studies on usage of Social media on youth

Chaudhary and Ali (2020)[9] studied the prevalence of Social media on youth. The study showed that prevalence of Social media was 31.6% .While comparing between females and males, females were found to be more addict than males.

Times of India(2020)[10] in article states that earlier in the times of Social media it was easy for the people to fing a partner using dating sites .But soon after the pandemic started the whole world is stuck in their homes .People who earlier used to enjoy physical dates have already started finding new ways to entertain themselves .Applications such as Tik Tok,Snapchat ,Instagram and Twitter has rapidly increased in quarantine times .The article states that users in order to validate their looks they dress up differently and look more presentable on Social media .But this change in dating methods also leads to fraud cases .

Sam (2019)[11] studies the use of Social media .They observed that political leaders use Social media to defame the reputation of their political rivals. Their studies were negative in their approach .They only talked about dark side of Social media .Social media also has strengthen the political participation of the public .

Bhattacharya(2018)[12] argues that the #metoo movement is an opportunity for the women across the globe to speak out against the predators. The organizations can ignore the complaint of single women but cannot ignore the complaint of the collective ones. While men are also a part of this movement but awareness programs must be held on how should men behave with the women. The movement is also hitting the Bollywood and other entertaining industries. The sexual predators are almost everywhere such as educational, public /private organizations. The author concluded that with the use of these smart technologies women facing assaults should scream loud and seek attention from public for help.

Khan(2018)[13] opines that Social networking sites like Facebook and MySpace etc. provides online platforms to the users to communicate and share information, create their attractive profiles and facilitates them to connect with people having similar interest .Social media platforms like these are a great way to establish relationships and also for social engagements .However, excessive use of these social platforms leads to psychological addiction amongst the users .The study suggests that it is crucial to acknowledge this psychological behavior which is affecting millions of people around the world .

Mills (2018)[14] in his study finds that selfie has a dangerous impact on young people especially women .It effects their mood and self-image. Although the picture filters help to, modify or beautify their pictures but it does not make them happy .Modifying their selfies women think more about their flaws and imperfections.

Sahu (2018)[15] studied that users of Online shopping prefer it because it is convenient to use and saves time and energy .Consumers opt for Online shopping sites such as Amazon, Flipkart and other sites because they get timely services and good quality products secure payment methods .The study concluded that up to date product information also increases the use of Online shopping .

Sisode (2018)[16] studied the relation between use of Facebook and self esteem. The study explored that Facebook use was high and self exteem amongst the users were low .The higher use of Facebook declined the face-to-face communication which increased loneliness and depression

Ifteekar (2017)[17] talks about impact of Snapchat on users and their interpersonal relationships .The study finds that users share their snaps with their family members, siblings and friends .It was observed that it develops new relationships .

Lal(2017)[18] opines that after the advent of Internet only few could have imagined its impact on the nation .In early 2000s the advent of Social media it has transformed Indian society .The shape and form of Social media has also changed multiple times. Social networking site such as Hi5 gave way to Myspace .After it success Orkut became famous which was made outmoded by Facebook.However, in todays times each platform has its own use .For eg.Instagram and Snapchat is sued for posting the pictures,for mocroblogging there is Twitter ,for having a long term message there is Facebook,for watching videos there is YouTube and daily chats are conducted on

WhatsApp.Social media has the capability to create a chaos in the society.However,like other technologies Social media also has negative points.Trolling and fake news is the main problem of Social media .Children today are being exposed to the virtual world .The author concludes that if Social media is used in a positive manner it offers its users various oppurtunities and possibilities.

Ali (2016)[19] in his study argues that Social media is a collection of applications that connect and link people to share information and keeps the people aware about the happenings and events of the entire world. From the initial stage it is in the state of progress. People of all age groups use Social media. It has made the world global village. People connect with each other through the platform of Social networking Sites can share their ideas and do video-conferencing. The author believed that it is helpful for students also. Students can interact on Facebook groups can can discuss topics of their choice. Platforms such as Facebook, Instagram and LinkedIn also facilitate to search for jobs. Various companies use it for the advertisement. The author conducted a study of 380 students and concluded that teenagers mainly use Social media for communication with friends and family .But it also has negative effects on culture and health.

Krishna(2016)[20] argues that as the advancement of technology is on rise it has also given its users new kind of addiction. The two main disorders are computer addiction and internet addiction. The basic tool nowadays to use internet is smartphone .These days they are equipped with highest resolution camera .The company claims that their phone gives the best picture. The biggest aim to take selfie is to post it online on their Social networking Profile such as Facebook, Twitter and LinkedIn. The author discusses that selfie is a double is a double-edged sword. Some people consider it as a way to boost up their self-confidence. People spend considerable amount of time to look good which helps them to boost their self-esteem. But the excessive selfie-taking is also considered as a mental disorder because people keep on paying attention to their looks and appearances. It can also lead to depression, voyeurism. The author concludes that the generations of smartphone use social media to not only maintain social relationships but also to maintain their personalities in an idealized way. On the sites such as Facebook and Instagram people portray themselves to look attractive .But taking regular selfie causes mental syndrome to its users. And only counseling and regular behavioral therapy can help.

Meikle (2016)[21] argues that Social media is used by millions of people and captures people's personal information and turns their daily lives into commercial data. He suggested that Facebook is the leading platform of sharing. Because of Facebook there is a new industry emerging -the sharing industry. There are several meanings of sharing-to impart information, to maintain relationships, to present a best version of self, to support something and someone and lastly to communicate with others. But in the world of new media share means to sell. The adoption of this industry by its users depends on the ways it is communicated to its users. The author talks about both the excitement and pleasure and fun linked with the use of Social media and also the problems attached with it. The author believes that the main feature of alternate media is convergence of everything i.e., the content, computing and communication. The content becomes digital and electronic devices such as computer, laptop and mobile phones are the basic platform to experience it.

Gaur (2015)[22] in his work gives an introduction of Social media and opines that on an average 47% of Social media users engage in the field of Social care. And also analyzed the effects of using Social media for new purpose. According to him, people nowadays, get their news from the internet rather than from newspapers or radio. He argues that for children also Social media helps in promoting creativity, interaction and learning and also helps them in doing their homework. He highlighted that Internet is a boon for the people. With the use of Internet free exchange of information, across the world can be done. This is all possible due to the advent of Social media. The most important feature of Social media is connecting the users with the other users. But extreme usage of it also makes a person feel depressed. People posts their pictures online and it is a pressure to post only the right picture in order to get likes. Because of these likes and share we are forced to project our best selves on the internet. He analyzed a concept called "Smiling depression" which means people who are depressed but do not show it. He concludes that Social media does more than bad. But everything has a good and bad aspect attached to it. Each individual should ensure that they use the platform in an appropriate manner.

Kurt (2015)[23] talks about the importance role of culture in society. It is the most important entity that a society can possess because it is responsible in shaping up the future and contains the societies present and past. In the era of technology it is possible to experience cultures another lifestyles. People can easily get information and share experience to other cultures by technology. He discusses that the culture is no more in the natural state now. It has already been modified. And as the technology will rise the modification of culture will continue. The author concludes that as a person will get more information on culture he would be aware of culture shock.

Verma (2015)[24] argues that the popularity of social networking sites has a humongous impact on the process of communication and interaction of the youth. Online communication is replacing the interpersonal communication and interaction .Although its users are constantly connected to each other but there are also risks which are associated with its use. The author discussed that Social networking sites provides a platform for the instant communication with the world. In other words, it helps in widening the relationship. But he also focused on its negative aspects such as stalking, bullying and privacy issues. The author concluded that the huge admiration of Social media has changed the concept of sociability amongst the youth. It is not only limited to interacting with the friends but also users can interact with the teachers and parents. The use of Social networking sites is associated with benefits such as feeling of connectedness, exploring new relationships and it also acts as source of information. But there are several risks associated with it such as cyber bullying and easy availability of illegal content. The author suggests that students should be aware of the ways of using Social media and the common risks associated with it.

Bevan (2014)[25] opines that Social networking sites provides the power to disclose important events and information on it. Self-disclosure on SNSs leads to continuing of friendship .The social group on Facebook is determined by the attitude and behavior of the user. The constant use of Facebook leads to relationship with the strangers who have similar thoughts. Information exchange will be high when a person will use Facebook at a high rate and it sometimes also reduces the chances of stress. The author argues that about 62% of adolescents use SNSs for communication in day-to-day life. However; the large number of friends' network gives psychological relief to its users.

Pauline (2014)[26] opines that the advancement of technology or internet has facilitated the swift emergence of complex interactions of dispersed group of people with common interests across the globe. The unique feature of virtual world or cyber community is its unusual compositions which are made irrespective of the global boundaries. The author argues that in the modern era, the process of socialization is done through mass media .Individuals learn the values and behavior of other groups through listening, watching and reading what other people do. He further concluded that the interactions done through Social networking Sites contributes to the emergence of new cultural expressions .While using Social networking sites people construct new slangs, new linguistic styles which are understandable to the millennial across the globe. Some online users also imbibe these new styles of writing to their offline situations such as mobile texting. This way it can be said that Social media shares popular culture. Social media also transmits the cultural heritage and is a popular platform for cultural diffusion.

Chambers (2013)[27] viewed that the SNS has contributed immensely to the intimacy, friendship and identity portraying by the people. He argued that due to the increasing use of social networking sites there is a drastic change in the various domains of the society. Due to the use of social media personal relationships are getting g stronger day-by-day .But on the other hand, his concern was also that whether these sites are wasting people's time and energy along with their mental peace. People are easily connected with each other. A person living in Australia can see his friend's new born baby who lives in India through the use of SNS .But also people who see their friends life activities on Facebook can get depressed after seeing their friends happening life on the facebook. This can disturb their mental life. He focused on the ways by which people make relationships on Social networking sites. He argued that it starts with normal friend requests and ends with strong bonds.

Schwartz(2012)[28] opines that earlier the adolescents were not having much Facebook friends. There were only those people who people used to know offline. People used to stay connected with friends every time with Facebook which also helped people to maintain offline relationship. The people sharing common interest were only added in their friends' lists. About 71% of the users felt that Facebook is a medium to maintain close relationships with friends. People also believed that users reveals true information about them through status update and profile pictures. Uers post their own profile pictures and tag their friends also on it which makes them feel important. But people feel secure and also prefer offline friendship rather online friendship. The author concluded that positive association with Facebook friends does not have any effect on the overall well-being. People do not easily accept the friend request of strangers.

Siapera (2012)[29] viewed that the advent of internet has given more opportunities to the people to interact with each other and make relation which are non-production .People use mobile phone and its facilities to fulfill their leisure/entertainment desires. In the virtual world no one knows about the person he/she is talking to. One can make his /her unique identity by creating any avatar of his/her choice.

Stieglitz(2012)[30] argued that the advent of Social media is on almost every aspect of the society. But majorly on communication and public discourse. Nowadays Social media is highly used in political context. Twitter is quintessential platform for the politicians who want to spread information and politically opinion publicly through Social media. Many political institutions, parties and political foundations have begun to use Facebook pages and groups for the purpose of entering into direct dialogue with citizens which encourages public discussions. It facilitates politicians and voters to directly interact with each other. During election times number of Facebook followers can be considered as an indicator of electoral success. Politicians who react on the comments of public and users are perceived more favourable. This leads to more transparency in political activities.

Ahn (2011)[31] focuses on the participation of youth in Social networking sites activities .Youth uses Social networking sites to start new relationships, interact with friends and colleagues and also to learn new skills. He highlights various questions such as-whether adolescent participation in Social networking sites gives them online harm or it helps them to develop new skills and relationships? Whether excessive use of Social networking sites troubles student's academics? He argues that now there is a need to talk about 'Social informatics' because how a person uses technology is influenced by the social forces and cultural norms. He argues that 'Warranting theories 'is based on the principle that people judge others on the basis of their social networking profile .Social networking sites helps them to develop new identities. He also talks about the digital divide which is prevalent in the modern society. If a student is deprived of using Social networking sites he will not be able to develop technical skills which will lead to lagging behind in this fast pace. He concludes that the use of Social networking sites helps them to develop new technical skills.

3.4 Research gaps

- Since there is no study on youth in Jaipur city regarding their use of Social media.

- Also, there are no studies assessing the role of Social media in creating a new youth Subculture.

Notes and references

1. Sulthana, A (2021),Usage of Social Media on purchase during Covid-19,

2. Joshi, S. (2019, April 21).Why millennial are signing up to party with strangers'. *The times of India,* pg.15.

3. Jalal,S(2018),Globalization and socio-cultural changes in India. *Language in India, 18(*8),247-265.

4. Kwan,L (2018),Culture, creativity and innovation, *Journal of cross cultural psychology, 49*(2),165-170.

5. Bhoje, G (2015), Indian Culture and Globalization, *International Journal of research in Engineering and Social sciences, 5*(5),50-64.

6. Domirani, T (2014), Investigation of the Cultural Impacts of Globalisation on the National Media (Television), *Current Research Journal of Social Sciences, 6*(2): 48-54.

7. Narsimhamurthy, N(2014),Cultural impact and gender on Indian young adults in using Social networking Sites. *International Journal of interdisciplinary and multidisciplinary studies,*1(7):113-125.

8. Ghosh, B (2011),Cultural changes and challenges in the era of Globalization: The case of India. *Journal of developing societies, 27*(2), 153-175.

9. Choudhury M. & Ali A. (2020). Social media addiction among youth: a gender comparison. International Journal of Indian Psychology, 8(3), 740-748.

10. Online dating: How the world of online dating transformed during the pandemic. (2020, November 15).Times of India.

11. Sam C, Thakurta P G (2019): The Real Face of Facebook in India, Delhi, Saurabh Printers, 33-45.

12. Bhattacharya, R.(2018).# Metoomovement: An awareness campaign. *International Journal of innovation,creativity and Change,3(4),* DOI: http://www.researchagte.net/publication/323816747.

13. Khan, N.T. (2018). Internet Addiction: A Global Psychological Addiction Disorder. The Journal of Medical Research, 2018; 4(4): 202-203.

14. Mills, J.(2018).''Selfie'' harm: Effects on mood and body image on young women. *Body image,* 27, 86-92.

15. Suman Sahu, S. D. (2018). Customer Satisfaction towards Online Shopping from Flipkart: With Special Reference to Raipur City. International Journal of Research in Engineering, Science and Management, 262-265.

16. Sisode, A. A. (2018). Facebook and self-esteem. International Journal of Indian Psychology, 6, 1.

17. I ftikhar,M.(2017).Virtual identities and Social media :A study of Snapchat . http://vfast.org/journals/index.php/VTSE@ 2017 ISSN(e): 2309-3951;ISSN(p): 2411-0221.

18. Lal,A.(2017).*India Social.*Gurugram,Hachette India.

19. Ali, A. (2016). Effects of Social media on youth: A case study in University of Sargodha. *International Journal of advanced research,*4,369-372.

20. Krishna,S(2016).Selfie syndrome: A disease of new era.*Research in pharmacy and health science,*2(2),118-121.

21. Meikle, G (2016), *Socialmedia: Communication, sharing and visibility,*Routledge, New York.

22. Gaur, S (2015),*Social media, Yking* books, Jaipur.

23. Kurt,I.(2015).Impact of Technology on the Perceptions of Culture Shock.*Mevlana International Journal of Moral and Values Education,*2(2),21-28

24. Verma,J.(2015).Impact of Social networking sites on social interaction-A study of college students. *International journal of humanities and Social sciences,*4(2),55-62

25. Bevan, J. L. (2014). Disclosures about important life events on Facebook: Relationships with stress and quality of life. *Computers in Human Behavior, 39*, 246-253.

26. Pauline,O.(2014). Social Media: Shaping and transmitting popular culture. *Covenant journal of communication,2*(1),93-108.

27. Chambers, D. (2013) *Social media and personal relationships: online intimacies and networked friendships.* New York: Palgrave Macmillan

28. Schwartz, S. (2012). Does Facebook Influence Well-Being and Self-Esteem Among Early Adolescents? Retrieved from Sophia, the St. Catherine University repository website: https://sophia.stkate.edu/msw_papers/91

29. Siapera, Eugenia (2012), *Understanding new media,Sage* publications, London.

30. Stieglitz,S(2012), Social media and political communication: a social media analytics framework. *Social Network Analysis and Mining,3*,1277-1291.DOI 10.1007/s13278-012-0079-3

31. Ahn,J (2011),The effects of Social networking sites on adolescents ,social and academic development :Current theories and controversies .*Journal of the American society for information science and technology ,62*(8),1435-1445.

CHAPTER: 4

RESEARCH METHODS

4.1 Introduction

Research methodology is the work done in this field, especially on the impact of Social media on youth. Therefore, the present study is undertaken to analyze the impact of Social networking sites on youth in creating a new culture amongst them in Jaipur city. It is believed that this study will throw lights on extent and magnitude of usage of social networking sites by the youth and the change it is bringing in the Indian culture.

More specifically the study has been undertaken to fulfill the aims and objectives given below.

4.2 Objectives

- To identify the extent of use of Social media amongst the youth of Jaipur city.

- To understand the role of social media in transforming the opinion of youth on various social institutions family, marriage, education and economy.

- To analyse the influence of social media on the behavioural aspect of youth.

- To understand whether new cultural patterns are emerging in Indian society due to the widespread use of Social media.

4.3 Research questions

Certain research question has been focused in the study and a trial has been made to answer these questions.

- What is the extent of usage of Social media amongst the youth?

- Whether these Social networking sites are transforming the opinion of youth on various social institutions such as family, marriage, education and economy?

- What is the impact of Social media in impacting the behavioural aspect of youth?

- Whether Social media is promoting new cultural patterns in Indian society?

4.4 Methodology

A well defined methodology, specific problem is stated clearly, particular areas of study are the characteristic of empirical study. In order to study any problem, the concepts given in that problem need to be defined clearly. Therefore, operational definitions of the concepts have been defined and stated below.

4.4(a) Operational definitions

Social networking sites- are the sites that help the users to create their profiles online through which they can make them enter into relationships and online exchanges.

Subculture-In the era of Social media ,Subculture can be defined as values, believes, practises and patterns of behaviour that are different from mainstream culture and that emerge and get fulfilled in the virtual space .It can be called as a culture which is virtual in nature and largely accepted and followed by younger generation .

Youth- Though according to National youth Policy youth is defined as those people aged between 15 to 29. Youth in the purpose of this study is taken as girls and boys aged between 18-30 .

4.4(b) Area, universe and sample

The area selected for the study is urban Jaipur city. It is selected because major educational and technological institutions are present here. Due to this many youngsters are present here. There fore; it is an accurate place to fulfil the purpose of studying the impact of Social media on youth.

Universe-The universe for the study consists of youth of Jaipur city. The population consists of youth between the age-group of 18-30 and users of Social media between the age –group of 40-50 .Purposive sampling is used. Purposive sampling is characterised by purposeful attempts to get sample which represents every aspect of sample .In the study who were active users of Social networking sites were included .The respondents were first asked their age, sex, occupation, religion and financial background .They were also asked about the extent they use Social media to analyse whether the use of Social networking is giving rise a to a new kind of subculture in Jaipur city.

Sample-A well defined questionnaire was given to the respondents .600 questionnaire was distributed but response collected were only 500 .Purposive sampling method was used .

4.4(c) Tools and techniques for data collection

Maximal effort has been done to collect data to maintain objectivity. The following tools have been used to study:

- **Questionnaire:** In order to collect first hand information, to compare data, a questionnaire was prepared .Thus questionnaire was filled by the respondents.

- **Unstructured interview:** As the study was qualitative in nature. The questions included in the questionnaire were not enough. So certain supplementary questions were also asked. The respondents were also given freedom to express their views also. Therefore unstructured interview is also helpful.

- **Secondary sources:** Sources like magazines, books and newspapers were also referred for the study.

4.5 Criteria for inclusion and exclusion

- Users in the age –group between 18-30 and 40-50 were included.

4.6 Criteria for exclusion

- Users who do not fall in the above age group were not included and also who do not use Social media was excluded.

4.7 Research ethics

- The researcher has maintained the anonymity of the respondents.

- No manipulation has been done with the facts and data received.

4.8 Limitations of the study

- The answers recorded by the respondents are taken as true.

- The most restrictive aspect in empirical study was the limitation of time, space and man power.

The qualitative methods used in this study have produced valuable results about the Social networking sites. These results can be used in the future as the basis of quantitative research through which the usage of social media in forming a new culture can be explored.

Notes and References

- Ahuja,R.(2001)*Research Methods*. Jaipur, Rajasthan: Rawat Publishers.

- Kothari, C. R. (2004). *Research Methodology: Methods and Techniques.* India: New Age International (P) Limited.

CHAPTER: 5
EMPIRICAL ANALYSIS

5.1 Introduction

The current society can also be termed as "information society "as internet and Social media have created information revolution world over, completely transforming societies .The advancement in information technology and wide spread use of Social media has made information accessible to almost all. The easy access to Smart phones and internet connectivity has made social media a common medium of communication and leisure in today's society .Geographical distances have become irrelevant and radical changes can be witnessed in the culture and lifestyle of all people particularly the youth. Social media has become an inseparable part of the life of youth which totally depends on the media for information about everything -the latest gadgets, fashion brands and latest models of cars etc. They even use social media platforms for voicing and forming their opinion on almost everything. The Indian youth is not an exception to this change and is an active Social media user .Social media has affected them in many ways both positive and negative .On the one hand, it gives a platform to the youth to express their ideas and opinions while on the other hand it is also leads to a feeling of inadequacy, lack of self-confidence ,depression, anxiety ,sleep deprivation etc. However, social media is here to stay and is the new normal for society and the youth both .Use of Social media is transforming the present Indian society and its impact can be seen most on the youth as a whole new culture is emerging due to its impact .The current study analyses the socio-cultural changes that have emerged due to social media amongst the youth of Jaipur city. In order to study the changes that have emerged due to the use of social media and in order to ascertain whether social media is giving rise to a new sub-culture, the study has been conducted on respondents belonging to two age groups. The study sample includes 500 respondents divided in the age group of 18-30(250 respondents) and 40-50 (250 respondents). The data has been collected by administering questionnaire to the respondents. In the first section, the demographic profile of respondents has been studied and in the second section, various changes and development in the Indian culture and society due to Social media, especially among the youth have been discussed.

5.2 Demographic profile

The demographic profile along with the various changes and development in Indian culture and society has been studied in thus chapter specifically on the youth.

5.2 Sex Composition

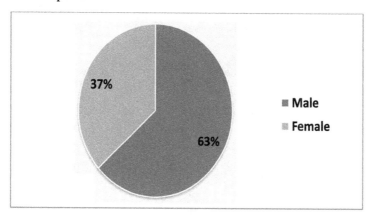

18-30 years

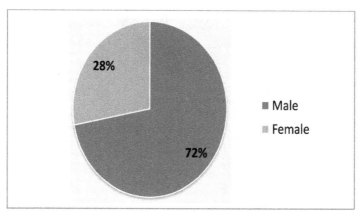

. 40-50 years

The sample consists of 500 respondents out of which 250 fall in the age group of 18-30 and 250 fall in the age group of 40-50. In the age group of 18-30,158 respondents are males i.e., 63 % of the population and 92 are females i.e., 37 % of the population.

5.2(ii) Religious affiliation

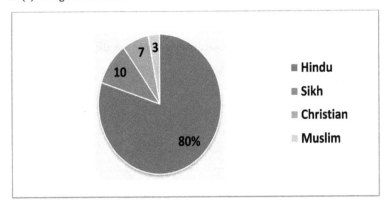

18-30 years

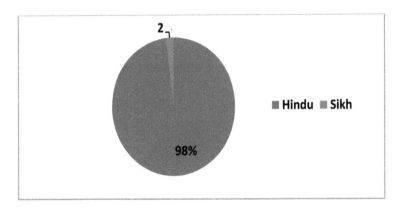

40-50 years

The respondents in the age-group of 18-30 belonged to different religions; Hindus formed the majority (80 %) followed by Sikhs (10 %), Christians (7 %) and Muslims (3%). Young practitioners of all the religions are active on Social networking sites. The number of Sikhs, Christians and Muslims is less as compared to Hindus owing to the fact that their overall population is less. In the age –group of 40-50, large number of respondents are Hindus and a very small %age of respondents are the Sikh population.

5.2(iii) Monthly family income

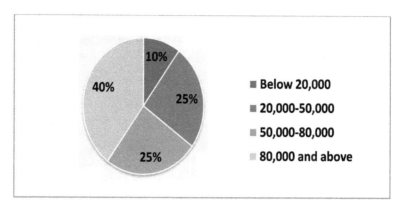

18-30 years

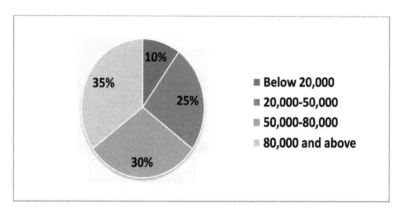

40-50 years

The data shows that in the age group of 18-30, 10% of the respondents fall in the income group of less than 20,000, 25% respondents fall in the income category of 20000-50000. Similarly, 25% of the respondents fall in the income group of 50,000-80,000 and 40 % of the respondents fall in the income category of 80,000 and above. The reason behind analyzing the income is to determine the basic socio- economic profile of the respondents. In the age group of 40-50, 10% respondents fall in the income category of less than 20,000, 25 % respondents belonged to the income range of 20000-50000 and 30 % of the respondents belonged to the income group of 50,000-80,000. However, 35 % belonged to the income range of 80,000 and above. The monthly family income was taken into consideration to determine whether the use of Social Media is dependent on the income levels.

5.2(iv) Occupation/designation (parents)

18-30 years   **40-50 years**

Occupation/designation (father) Occupation/designation (father)

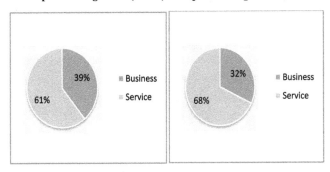

Occupation/designation (mother) Occupation/designation (mother)

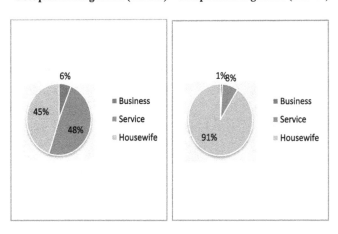

Maximum number of younger respondents have working parents, where both are either doing business or are in service. 45 % answered that their mothers are home makers. The absence of both the parents during the day cannot be eliminated as one of the factors for increased online social activity as young respondents seek human interaction through virtual means to combat loneliness. Another important factor to consider is that parents with higher disposable income can afford more gadgets for their family, which means that people will have multiple means of accessing social media and easier ways to do so. In contrast 91 % of the respondents in the age group of 40-50 said that their mother was a housewife which implies that they had access to both parental interaction and parental supervision at home while growing up.

5.3 Availability of technological devices at home

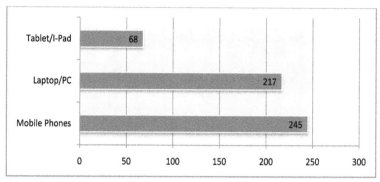

18-30 years

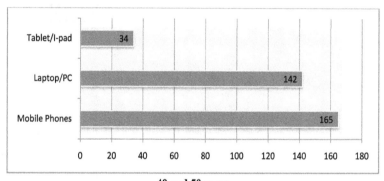

40 and 50 years

Respondents in the age group of 18-30 have more technological devices at home which points towards a greater desire for connectivity and an easier means to do so. Respondents in the younger age group own mobile phones which is the most popular device for using social media sites. New age gadgets are equipped with internet which has brought a paradigm shift in performing everyday tasks .Smartphone facilitates the users to access enormous information at fingertips .On one hand it helps in staying connected with each other but also adversely affects the face-to-face relations with the family members. The respondents in the age group of 40-50 have fewer devices at home in comparison to their younger counterparts. But this doesn't mean they don't own any technological devices, most of them have at least one gadget at home that can be used to access social media sites. The prominent functions of the Internet such as instant messaging, blogs, chat, bulletin boards and social networking sites, made it popular among adolescents. Moreover, they are called as 'digital netizens' and use social networking sites to connect online.

5.4 Extent of usage of Social media

5.4(i) Member of Social networking Sites

18-30 years

40-50 years

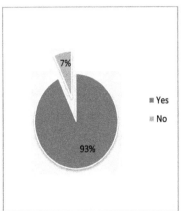
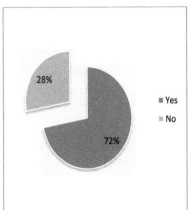

93 % respondents from the age-group of 18-30 are the members of Social networking sites while 7% respondents do not use Social media .The easy availability of internet and the easy access to mobile phones is the foremost reason to use Social media as it is easy to use platforms such as Facebook, Twitter and Instagram etc. on mobile phones. Another reason for using Social media is that it keeps them updated with the latest news of their family and friends and even with the latest events around the world. In the age group of 40-50, 72% respondents use Social media which is less as compared to the generation of 18-30. 28% respondents do not use Social networking sites. 72% respondents in the age group 40-50 consist of high-ranking professionals who use Social networks such as LinkedIn for professional opportunities or Sites like Twitter which helps them to stay abreast with the latest updates. Facebook is claimed to be the most used site for browsing news online .Respondents in the age group of 40-50 are less interested in posting selfies they rather enjoy updating their timeline by reading articles, photos and videos related to their interest .

5.4(ii) **Reasons for not being a member of Social networking Sites**

18-30 years   **40-50 years**

35% respondents in the age-group of 18-30 are not interested in joining Social media. 10 % respondents also believe that Social media is full of inappropriate content because people post almost everything on Social media like what they eat, wear, and how they feel .Earlier it was believed that eating should be done in private but now people post pictures of their food on social media. Also 35% respondents have privacy issues with social media as whatever is posted on Facebook or Instagram immediately becomes viral. Personal data is also visible to people and can be misused. Similarly, in the age group 40-50, about 24% respondents have no idea what social media is. This is because respondents of this age group are busy in their office and family relationships and do not have enough time to be on Social media .34% respondents are not interested in joining Social media and state that it is meaningless and unnecessary. 10% of the respondents joined it to contact and communicate with friends, family and colleagues etc. but later it changed to a time consuming activity .32 % respondents opine that it is full of inappropriate content which is not rendering any good to society.

5.4(iii) **Means to access Social Media**

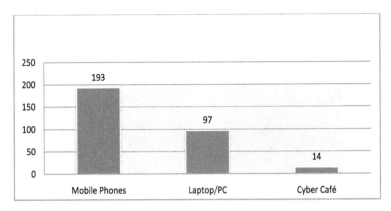

18-30 years

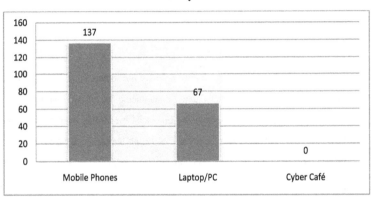

40 -50 years

In the above figure, 77.2% respondents prefer to use social media through their phones. While PC is also a preferred means by 38.8% respondents, cyber cafes are popular with only a few. The reason for this is that mobile phones provide an easier and cheaper way to access internet while laptops may not be a feasible option for everyone. Though Cyber Café were popular for a little while some years ago, these days people rarely go to cyber cafes and can easily access social media through their phones instead. Similarly, in the age group of 40-50, 54.8% people use Social media on their mobile phones. With growing internet access through phones visit to cyber cafes has almost become negligible.

5.4(iv) Major Social networking Sites used

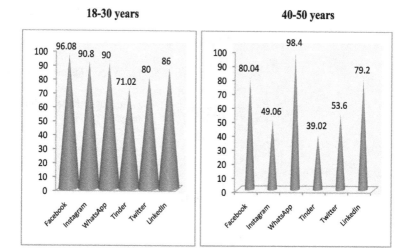

(Figures overlap because respondents have given more than one answer)

The above figure indicates that Facebook is perhaps the most popular texting app amongst the respondents of age group 18-30 with 96.08% respondents using it. The main reason for using it is that it is a platform for self-presentation. Instagram is a close favorite with 90.8 % users. It gives its users the opportunity to showcase their photography skills. Users also use different filters to make their pictures more attractive. Also it facilitates its users to beautify their pictures. 90 % respondents use WhatsApp. 71.02 % respondents use Tinder. 80 % respondents use Twitter. 86 % respondents use LinkedIn. In the age group of 40-50 WhatsApp is the majorly used site amongst the youth with 98.4 % respondents using it. Facebook is the second favorite with 80.4 % respondents while 79.2 % respondents use LinkedIn .Some social networking sites like WhatsApp even facilitate the users to make video calls.

5.4(v) Effect on family interaction

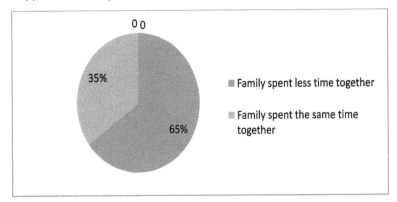

18-30 years

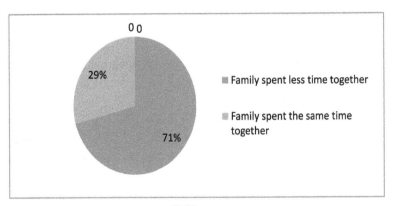

40-50 years

It has been found that 65 % respondents in the age group of 18-30 have been spending less time with family members after joining Social media while 35 % respondents claim that there has been no change in their family schedule after joining Social media as they spend same amount of time with them .In the age group of 40-50, 71 % respondents claim that after joining Social media families spend less time together and 29 % respondents feel that the time spent together is the same. Social media keeps its users busy in front of a screen; users have more difficulty in understanding emotions and maintain relations. Excessive use of Social media is resulting in reduced interpersonal face-to-face interaction resulting in loneliness, anxiety and depression. This is because despite physical proximity, the communication has reduced drastically .Change in the interaction patterns can be observed which marks as a development of cultural change.

5.4(vi) Personal Information on Social networking profile

18-30 years   **40-50 years**

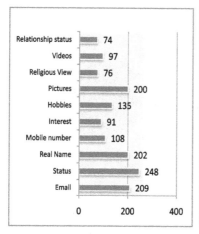 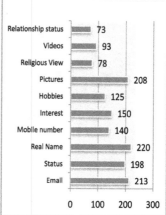

29.2 % (73) respondents in the age group of 18-30 freely post their relationship status or pictures with their partners on Social networking profile. Approx. 37.2 % respondents openly post personal and other kind of videos on Social media . The respondents of both the age group share their political and religious views on social networking sites. Such behavior not only indicates social trust but also civic engagement and political participation. The above data clearly shows that people are not worried about disclosing their beliefs and personal information online. Respondents of both age groups freely share their views regarding different matters, post pictures and videos, talk about their interests etc. and often seek validation/ attention in the form of likes, shares etc. Even details like personal email address and phone numbers are shared without much thought. This might be one of the reasons for increased cyber crimes but this kind of participation lying as it makes it easier for culprits to target people. Freely available information also makes it easier for people to stalk others as almost everything about a person's life is posted on their profile.

5.4(vi) Reasons for using Social networking Sites

18-30 years   **40-50 years**

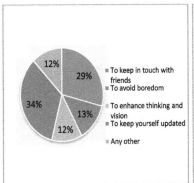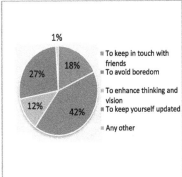

34% respondents in age group of 18-30 use social media because they wish to remain updated. Social platforms let them know about what's happening in their surroundings, the current status of their favorite celebrities, employment updates, new tends, etc. 42% respondents in the age-group of 40-50 uses social media as a method to pass time and avoid boredom. This difference shows that for the younger generation social media is a way of life whereas for the older generation it is more a means of entertainment. 29% respondents in the age group of 18-30 and 18% in the age group of 40-50 uses social media to keep in touch with others, which implies that the primary objective of social media, i.e. human connectivity, is of lesser importance to the respondents. 12 % respondents see social media as a platform to enhance their thinking and vision. While use of social media is limited to conventional sense in the older age group, around 12% respondents of 18-30 age bracket use social media for other things also, like, playing games, making money through youtube channels and instagram promotions, learning various skills etc.

5.4(vii) Status update generally pertains to

18-30 years

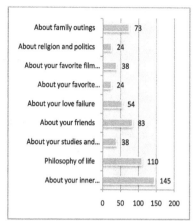

40-50 years

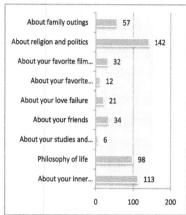

(Figures overlap because respondents have given more than one answer)

In the age group of 18-30 88 % respondents post their real name on Social media profile post their inner thoughts on their Social media profile .Because they think that it is best platform to showcase their inner feelings about whether they feel happy or sad. In this current scenario, as everybody is free to express their views .Users post almost everything on Social media .People post about the happenings in the world. It conveys other people current mood, current location and current activity etc. Similarly in the 40-50 age group majority of people post about their inner thoughts .Sites such as Twitter enables its users to post their views on anything .This also creates cold war amongst various communities, groups and religious peoples.

5.5 Role of Social media in transforming the opinion of youth on various Social institutions

5.5(i) Participation in political activities/discussions on Social media

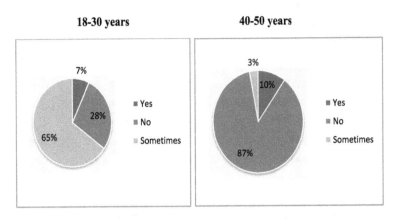

65% respondents in the age group of 18-30 sometimes participate in the political discussions on Social media. They occasionally share political opinions, retweet posts or links to the political contents. By contrast 28% respondents never participate in the political discussions online. 7 % respondents participate in the political discussions on Social media .13% respondents in age group of 40-50 participate in the political discussions or comments .Respondents follow few politically active persons on Twitter, Facebook and Instagram .87% respondents do not participate in online political discussion or post comments because they are of the opinion that this adds stress to already fraught political discussions. 3 % respondents sometimes participate in the political discussions online .Twitter gives opportunity to its users to post views using hashtags .Sites like Facebook, Twitter and Instagram has become political communication channel .At the time of election it gives voters the opportunity to interact directly with each other .Platforms such as Blogs facilitates users to interact with politically similar people that leads to citizens views into strong motivation for political parties. The increasing use of social media gives more transparency and also facilitates the citizens to get involve in decision making process.

5.5(ii) Educational option on Social media

18-30 years   40-50 years

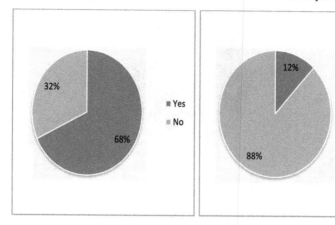

68% respondents in the age group of 18-30 years use social media for educational purposes. The study indicated that Sites such as Facebook, Twitter and Instagram etc. facilitate the students, teachers and parents for getting information while they connect with e-learning groups, notes and class assignments which are updated on it by the teachers. YouTube gives the opportunity to the students to benefit themselves through online tutorial exercises .Some colleges and universities also offer online courses and program's which are shared through social communities .In the age group of 40-50, 88% respondents indicated that it is just a waste of time and also distracts the students from studying .Learning face-to-face helps the students to interact with each other .Regular attendance helps them to learn discipline and follow regular schedule .

5.5(iii) Social media for employment opportunities

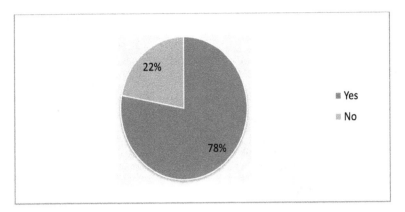

18-30 years

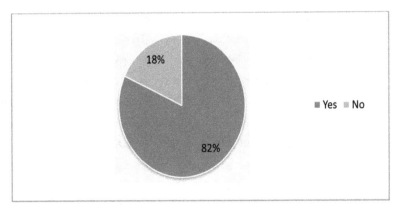

40-50 years

In the above figure, 78% respondents in the age –group of 18-30 use Social media for employment opportunities. Sites such as LinkedIn, Facebook and other Social networking sites acts as search engine to search jobs .In the age group of 40-50 82% of the respondents also considers and uses Social media as a platform to search employment opportunities .Social media is a platform which is used for connecting and sharing photos, videos and posts with each other .But sites like LinkedIn, Monster.com and Facebook etc. facilitates its users to solve purposes like professional and career prospective purposes .The new way of searching for jobs will definitely lead to proper, effective and efficient use of human resources .

5.5(iv) Use of apps which facilitate buying and selling

18-30 years

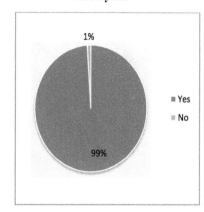

40-50 years

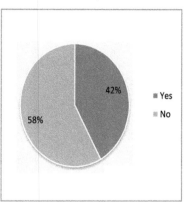

A study conducted in Jaipur city concludes that buying behavior is changing rapidly among youth of Jaipur city and is largely based on Social media (Chaturvedi:2017)[1.] In the figure, 99% respondents from the age group of 18-30 uses Online shopping sites .They prefer buying products from the shopping sites such as Myntra, Amazon and so on .Facebook and Instagram also has the feature to buy and sell products .Also they can share the product information with their friends, family and siblings etc. Younger generation use Social media to research what they want to buy. While in the age group of 40-50 years only 42% respondents uses online shopping sites. They have fear of giving their personal details and also are not sure whether they are buying it from the direct store. Also shopping online delays their joys of purchasing. 58% respondents prefer traditional methods of shopping because it facilitates them to touch and try the product.

5.5(v) Views on marriage

18-30 years　　　　　　　　　　**40-50 years**

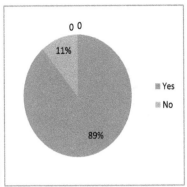

51% respondents in the age group of 18-30 do not want to get married. 49% respondent prefer marriage. Forsome, career and freedom are important for them. Also, commitment is scary and casual dating is the best alternative .Youngsters find marriage a mere "tag" nowadays, various social media bloggers and influencers have changed the mindset of young individuals. Most of them want to get into a live in relationships now without giving it an official name tag through marriage. The idea of marriage is pressurizing for them as they feel obligated to live with the same partner for their entire life. Whereas, in a live-in, they can set themselves free as and when they realize that things are not working well for them. Accessibity to apps like Tinder, Happn and truly madly provide an easier option for hook ups. Since in the age group of 40-50 89 % respondent prefer marriage over live-in relationships. Marriage is an institution which legally and socially bonds the individual with each other. However, it can also be concluded that Social media has become a powerful force in shaping marital decisions for youngsters.

5.5(vi) Views on procreation

18-30   **40-50**

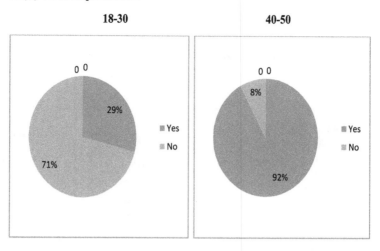

71 % respondents in the age group of 18-30 are against procreation. They find it important to pursue their career rather than to have children and compromise .They believe procreation can create hurdles in their professional lives. 29 % respondents believe that procreation is important.92 % respondents in the age group of 40-50 opines that it is important to procreate and have children .Social media is also responsible in promoting such ideas by publishing posts that are anti-natal and propagate moral movement of this nature.However, there were respondents who want to have children .They want to have stable families as they consider family as the most important social institution.

5.6 Time spent on Social media

5.6 (i) Time spent on Social media

18-30 years   **40-50 years**

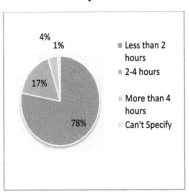

55 % respondent claims to use Social media for 2-4 hours, 25 % respondents use Social media for less than 2 hours. From this it is clear that though social media is a visible part of people's life these days, it isn't an inescapable addiction for most. 17% in older bracket indicates that social media has become an integral part of people's life nowadays. It is concerning that in the 18-30 age brackets, around 10% use social media for more than 4 hours and another 10% are unable to specify how much time they spend online. This means that there are some sections of the younger generation that perhaps need to reassess their social media habits. This overuse or perhaps dependency is prevalent in only a few in the age group of 40-50 respondents. 78% of respondents in the age group of 40-50 use Social media for less than 2 hours .Social media offers its users variety of things to do .By just scrolling their phone screen or Facebook, Instagram timeline they can keep a check on their friends, family and colleagues, cope up with boredom, stalk anyone, find a right outfit for a party or become famous .It is a kind powerful marketing machine working at the background which influences the daily activities .

5.6(ii) Accessing Social media during late hours

<table>
<tr><td align="center">18-30 years</td><td align="center">40-50 years</td></tr>
</table>

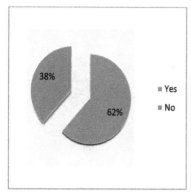 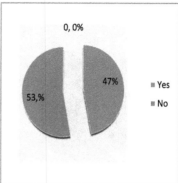

In the above figure, 62 % respondents access Social media at night while 38 % respondents do not use Social media at night. In the age group of 40-50 47 % respondents use Social media at night and 53% respondents do not use Social media at night. This includes constant checking of other person's last seen status/activity, latest trends/updates on social media. It has also been found that a social media account keeps them eager about the next activity which is about to happen on social media. This creates a fear of losing out/missing out of events for an individual which may have/had happened. The regular usage of their respective social media accounts i.e. Instagram, Whatsapp and Facebook keeps them anxious and subconsciously active and therefore it deeply impacts their mental state and dreams. Browsing internet during the night is one of the cause of insomnia .It may impact the quality of sleep and can also increase the risk of depression. The impact on sleep quality can even affect the functioning of the next day. Late night use of Social media increases levels of daytime sleepiness and impaired functioning of the students. It also tends to worsen mood by creating a feeling of wasted time. However, in the age group of 40-50 47 % respondents use Social media .The possible reason for the same is that the respondents of this age group are mature enough to take care of their health and are also aware of the associated health risks and hence avoid the temptation.

5.7 Impact of Social media on behavioral aspect of youth

5.7(i) Social media affecting your Social life

18-30 years	40-50 years

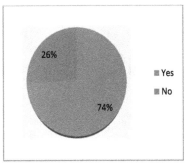 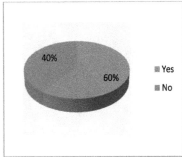

74 % respondents feel that Social networking affects their social life in both positive and negative way .Because of Social media youngsters spend maximum time on Social networking sites .Through Social media users are connected to their friends and family members who live far, but also they are disconnected with the people who live with them in the same place .In other words it can be said that Social media has caused them loss of direct communication or face-to-face communication with friends and relatives. They are often busy in looking at the screens .In the age group of 40-50 60 % respondents claims that Social media affects their Social life .Respondents feel that Social media has created an environment of information, communication and interconnectivity .Users give priority to communicate with Social media friends over career commitments .

5.7(ii) Self presentation on Social media

18-30 years   **40-50 years**

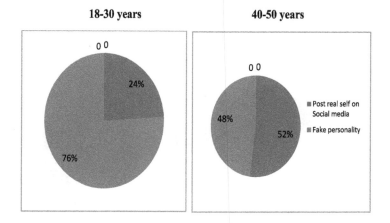

24 % respondents in the age group of 18-30 post their real self on Social media and 76% agree that they post their fake personality or share the pictures which are most attractive and bring popularity and likes to their profile. However, in the age –group of 40-50 48 % respondents on Social media share their real self on Social media and 48 % respondents portray their fake personality on Social media. Self presentation is generally considered to be motivated by a desire to make a favorable impression on others, or an impression that corresponds to one's ideals. This trend indicates the process of *'self commodification'* (Siibak, 2010)[2]. Getting positive feedsback in terms of "likes and comments" raises their self esteem .But also negative comments on their pictures have serious phycosocial consequences .Moreover, people compare their appearance with others which also ledas to depression.(O'Keefe et al., 2011)[3].

5.8 Role of Social media in creating new lifestyle patterns

5.8 (i) Use of social media for updating wardrobe

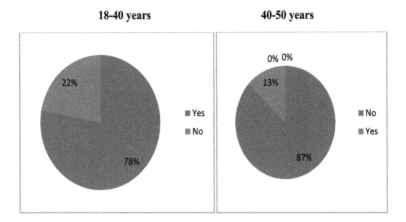

In the above figure, 78% respondents amongst the age group of 18-30 opine that Social media impacts their wardrobe selection and their dressing style also .Social media is the easiest tool to communicate new ideas .Fashion industry also claims that it is the easiest way to communicate with the customers. Youngsters nowadays can easily see fashion blogs, catwalk shows and main fashion weeks at different platforms such as Facebook, Instagram and etc. 22% respondents never get influenced by Social media for updating their wardrobe. However, in the age –group of 40-50, 87% respondents never use Social media for updating their wardrobe only 13% respondents refer to their favorite fashion designer or stylist to update their dressing style or wardrobe.

5.8(ii) Use of emoticons /acronyms while talking on SNS

18-40 years   **40-50 years**

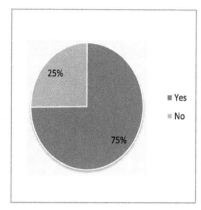 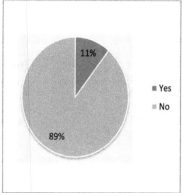

In the figure, 75% respondents in the age –group of 18-30 use emoticons and acronyms for communicating through Social media while 25 % respondents do not use them. In the age –group of 40 – 50,11% respondents use emoticons and acronyms while talking through Social media .The use of acronyms like TTYL, OMG, and LOL indicate how Social media is lessening long and cumbersome phrases. The reason behind using emoticons is the feeling that emoticons, smileys and acronyms can convey their messages meaningfully. Use of emoticons gives them a feeling of real conversations. It also lightens the mood by enhancing sarcasm and humour. Emoticons are thus emerging as a new language being used primarily by the youth and other users. The use of emoticons and acronyms also communicates the crux of meaning or emotion better than formal language .However in the age group there are majority of users i.e., 89% respondents who do not use emoticons and acronyms while chatting because they feel it makes the conversation more confusing and also destroys formal language .The fact that a large section of youth is using emoticons denotes a rise in alternate communication genres.

5.8 (iii) Reading preferences

18-30 years   **40-50 years**

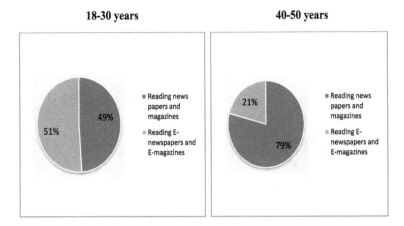

49% respondents in the age –group of 18-30 use Social media and other e-newspaper applications to keep themselves informed and updated .Digitalization helps in getting live updates about the happenings of the world by just one click. Respondents were of the opinion that digital magazines and newspapers are less expensive and can be accessed anytime and anywhere. However, in the age –group of 40-50, 79% respondents prefer reading and listening to news through traditional sources, while only 21% respondents in this age group prefer reading e-newspapers or accessing Social media platforms.They are of the opinion that online news is not comprehensive and does not disseminate quality information.

5.8(iv) Physical Fitness and Gaming preferences

18-30 years   40-50 years

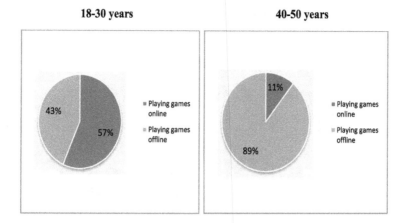

57% respondents prefer playing online games. In this technological era, where internet is cheap and easily available, there is easy access to online games. Games such as Ludo king, Pub-G, etc. are popular amongst the youngsters now. Only 43% of the respondents prefer offline games and outdoor sports with the family members, friends and siblings. Researches indicate that addiction to online games is the main cause of loneliness, depression and anxiety. However, In the age –group of 40-50, only 11% of respondents prefer playing online games while 89 % of the respondents prefer playing offline games with their family members .They believe that playing with family strengthens bonds and promotes understanding and cooperation. Besides, offline games such as ludo, chess, and various outdoor games such as badminton, cricket going gym also keeps physically fit and active.

5.8(v) Social media as a platform to display daily activities

18-30 years   40-50 years

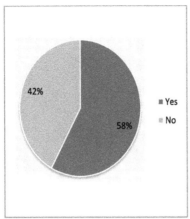
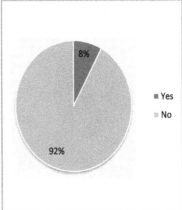

The above figure shows that 58% respondents from the age–group of 18-30 use Social media to publish their daily activities such as what they eat, wear, places they visit and shows they watch etc. while 42% do not use Social media to display their lifestyle. 92% respondents in the age –group of 40-50 are of the opinion that they never use Social media to showcase their life .They are of the opinion that it is a waste of time .and it also creates a feeling of hatred, depression and anxiety amongst other friends. It is can be said that sharing life on social media is a sure sign of deep need of recognition. But, in an article published in Science News, it was highlighted that posting on social media plays a dual role. On the one hand, it helps in recalling, evaluating and sharing with others memories of personal experiences while on the other hand, it helps in the construction of the self by shaping the way we remember one remembers his experiences. However, the selection of memories is not an individual act but through an external resource like Facebook. The study sheds new light on memory theories and have important implications for the construction of *"the autobiographical self"* in the internet era where the virtual externalisation of personal memories has become commonplace"

5.8(vi) The selfie culture

18-30 years   **40-50 years**

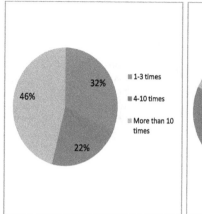
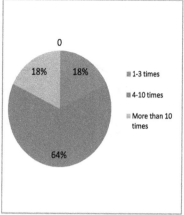

46 % respondents in the age group of 18-30 years take selfie for more than 10 times a day while 32 %take selfie 4-10 times a day and 22 % take selfie 1-3 times a day. 64 % respondents in the age group of 40-50 years take selfie 4-10 times a day, 18 % take selfie 1-3 times a day and 18 % respondents take selfie for more than 10 times a day. Clicking selfies and sharing them on Social networking sites like Instagram, Facebook, Snapchat is indicative of self-expression. Selfies are taken for a wide variety of reason. According to some, they are taken to celebrate an occasion or a moment or to share an event or achievement; while for others, it is symbols of narcissism. Selfies have become the new way to document lives.

5.8(vii) Dating preferences

18-30 years	40-50 years

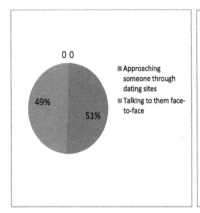

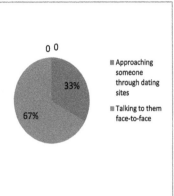

51% respondents in the age group of 18-30 prefer approaching someone through dating sites, 49 % respondents prefer talking to them face-to-face. In the age group of 40-50, 33 % respondents prefer approaching someone through dating sites and 67 % respondents prefer talking to them face-to-face. With multiple dating apps and wide social media platforms, meeting new people for striking a romantic connection is becoming both accessible and desirable. Dating has acquired a new dimension as the process is screen based but still youngsters and the respondents between the age–group of 40-50 years prefer approaching someone through face-to-face interaction as they feel that in person relations lead to stronger bonds ,build trusts and are long lasting .

5.8(viii) Imitation of lifestyle patterns of celebrities

18-30 years   **40-50 years**

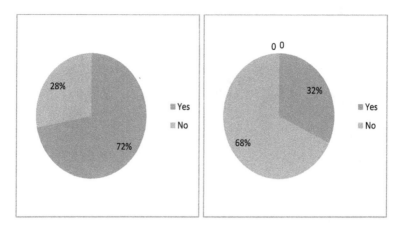

72 % in the age group of 18-30 use Social media to stalk their favorite celebrities' lifestyle patterns. Majorly used Social networking sites is Instagram. 68 % respondents in the age group of 40-50 have no interest in stalking celebrities on Social media .Respondents not only stalk their favorite celebrities on Social media but also try to transform themselves by imitating their lifestyles and activities. Advent of Social media has changed the idea of leisure .Bicycle tours, nature activities, swimming and various outdoor activities which were previously considered leisure now being replaced by the use of Social networking sites.

Importance of Social media

18-30 years   40-50 years

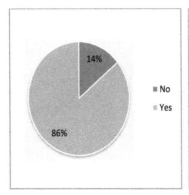
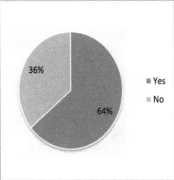

In the above figure 1.20, 86% respondents in the age –group of 18-30 are of the opinion that Social media is important to them because it reduces their feeling of loneliness, helps them to develop new social skills, strengthens their friendships, for users it is also a place to seek support and most important of all it helps them to keep updated. Similarly, In the age group of 40-50 ,64% respondents are of the opinion that Social media is important for them .The foremost reason is that it keeps them updated about the happenings around the world and they can easily pos their views and ideas on any topic and situations. 36% respondents are of the opinion that social media is of less importance for them .It is a waste of time and creates a feeling of depression, anxiety and loneliness and also capable of creating cold war in certain situations.

Notes and References

1. Chaturvedi, S. (2017).An effect of Social media on the youth buyer behavior for apparels in Jaipur City :A study .*IJBARR,2(5),163-171.*

2. Siibak, A., 2010. Constructing masculinity on a social networking website. The case-study of visual self-presentations of young men on the profile images of SNS Rate.ee. Young.18 (4),403-425.

3.   O'Keeffe, G. S., Clarke-Pearson, K., 2011. Clinical Report – The impact of social media on children, adolescents and families. American Academy of Pediatrics. 800-804.

CPSIA information can be obtained
at www.ICGtesting.com
Printed in the USA
BVHW071944290123
657300BV00014B/1197

9 781965 893623